The Lutheran Course
Leader Book

ABOUT THE LUTHERAN COURSE

The story of this course begins with *The Lutheran Handbook* (Augsburg Fortress, 2005), a field guide to church stuff, everyday stuff, and Bible stuff. The handbook is a guide to Lutheran theology and culture, as well as the innovative learner resource for Here We Stand confirmation. Nearly 90,000 copies were sold in the first six months after its release. Confirmation students, teachers, and pastors read the handbook and told parents and others about it. Adults read the handbook and started asking, "Is there a course for us that's based on *The Lutheran Handbook*?"

Well, you asked for it and here it is—The Lutheran Course!

ABOUT "WINKING LUTHER"

If you haven't read or seen *The Lutheran Handbook* yet, don't worry. The icon of Martin Luther winking at the reader gives you a glimpse into the handbook and The Lutheran Course.

Luther's theology is grounded in paradoxes—sinner/saint, law/gospel, hidden/revealed—and illuminated by a down-to-earth, everyday sense of humor. "Winking Luther" combines the serious, formal scholarship that was his life's work with the humor and lightheartedness that characterized his personality.

The wink on Luther's face indicates that, even though theology is serious stuff, we should nonetheless remember that it is not our theology that saves us, but Jesus Christ. Our life in the church, therefore, can be buoyant, and our theological wranglings can be done with a sense of humor and love for our neighbor.

The Lutheran Course
Leader Book

Augsburg Fortress
Minneapolis

THE LUTHERAN COURSE
LEADER BOOK

Copyright © 2005 Augsburg Fortress. All rights reserved. Except for brief quotations in critical articles or reviews or the reproducible sheets found on pages 99–110, no part of this book may be reproduced in any manner without prior written permission from the publisher. Write to: Permissions, Augsburg Fortress, Box 1209, Minneapolis, MN 55440.

Scripture quotations are from *New Revised Standard Version Bible*, copyright © 1989 Division of Christian Education of the National Council of the Churches of Christ in the United States of America. Used by permission.

Thank you to all the congregations, pastors, group leaders, and adult learners who contributed to this project by requesting a course like this or field-testing the material.

Writers: Mark D. Johns, Ken Sundet Jones
Editors: Gloria E. Bengtson, Laurie J. Hanson, Rebecca Lowe, Kristofer Skrade
Cover Design: Laurie Ingram
Interior Design: Rebecca Lowe
Cover Art: Spunk Design Machine
Interior Art: Brenda Brown

ISBN-13: 978-0-8066-5277-1
ISBN-10: 0-8066-5277-2

Also available:
The Lutheran Handbook. ISBN 0-8066-5179-2
The Lutheran Course Workbook. ISBN 0-8066-5278-0
The Lutheran Course Starter Kit. ISBN 0-8066-5290-X
The Lutheran Course DVD. ISBN 0-8066-5276-4

The paper used in this publication meets the minimum requirements of American National Standard for Information Sciences—Permanence of Paper for Printed Library Materials, ANSI Z329.48-1984.

Manufactured in the U.S.A.

CONTENTS

Introduction: The Family Reunion	7
Setting Up The Lutheran Course	10
Your Role as the Large Group Leader	14
Session 1 How to Tell the Difference Between the Law and the Gospel	20
Session 2 Five Things You Should Know about the Lutheran Reformation	26
Session 3 The Anatomy of a Baptism	32
Session 4 How to Receive Communion	38
Session 5 The Three Most Rebellious Things Jesus Did	44
Session 6 How to Read the Bible	50
Session 7 How to Share Your Faith with Someone	56
Presenters	62
Transcripts	63
Small Group Leader's Guide	99
Session 1 Handout	101
Table Talk Pages	102
Course Evaluation Form	110

INTRODUCTION

The Family Reunion

Mark D. Johns

When I was a kid, a highlight of the summer was the family reunion. My dad was one of nine children, all with spouses and families of their own, which made for a pretty large crowd when they all gathered at Grandpa and Grandma's house for a weekend get-together. There were shouting cousins running and chasing all over the place! Grandma coordinated tons of food, and Grandpa's main job was teasing grandkids. The grown-ups mostly sat and talked, and shared news of what was happening in their lives at home, at work, and in their churches.

The family reunion was a great time, but it was on the way home, with just our little nuclear (but not radioactive) family in the car, that we could talk about what had happened and give the experience some perspective. "Why was Aunt Debra crying so much?" "How come Cousin Fred always has to have his own way?" "Did you see how much beer Uncle Jon was drinking?" On that ride home my parents would try, patiently and simply, to explain very large, grown-up things—like what an alcoholic is, and what a divorce is all about, and how those things cause struggles for children. On the ride home we would laugh again at Grandpa's jokes, compare experiences, and giggle about how Cousin Jen held hands with her new boyfriend the whole day.

The family reunion was great fun, a wonderful experience, a sensory overload with too much to see, to hear, to taste, and to experience. The reunion was songs and laughter and teasing and food. The ride home was a dialog and conversation in which all that we had seen and heard and experienced was discussed until it began to make some sense. The ride was an opportunity, in the intimate safety of a small car, to sit quietly in the back seat listening to what the adults were saying to each other in the front seat, and a chance to ask questions that would have been much too embarrassing to ask when surrounded by a large family gathering.

The Lutheran Course, like a family reunion, is designed to include both the whole family gathering and the ride home.

The large group gathering is energized. It's singing and jokes and fun and listening to Grandpa's stories. A perfectly Lutheran thing to do would be to start with a potluck supper or some other sort of refreshments (food is always very Lutheran, especially if there's flavored gelatin). As people arrive, there should be lots of talk and sharing news of what is happening in people's lives at home, at work, and in church. The gathering time begins light and lively, then may even get a bit rowdy, especially if you've got a good song leader. But the large group gathering of the family reunion soon enough settles down to business, and the business at hand is a listening to Grandpa's stories. In this case, "Grandpa" is one of the teachers of the faith who visits electronically on video (despite the fact that not all of them are male, nor are all of them old enough to be grandparents).

But there's also the ride home—a time with a smaller group of people that have the opportunity to get to know one another well, to trust one another, and, perhaps on a good day, even to love one another just a bit. They don't have to talk in a car (that can be saved for the actual ride home—this is more of a "virtual" ride home). They should meet in a Sunday school room or some other safe, quiet space that is a short walk from where the large gathering took place. But more importantly, this group should be small enough that they *could* all fit in a car together if they had to. There should be at least three or four, but six or seven is the maximum.

Someone in the small group should get the ball rolling. The pages in the workbook will help. But the whole point of the ride home is that everyone gets to put in his or her two cents worth: no opinion is too absurd, no question is stupid. Everyone talks, everyone listens, people respond to one another. That same someone who gets the ball rolling should keep order (well, keep chaos to a minimum), and make sure everyone gets a chance to speak up or ask questions. But mostly it's freewheeling conversation about what went on at the big reunion that night. When members of the small group get tired of talking, they can pile in a car together and go out for ice cream. Or they can wash the car together instead, if they'd rather. Meeting outside of class is encouraged, but never mandatory.

The purpose of the large group gathering is to get people stimulated to talk, and to establish an intriguing topic for them to talk about. The purpose of the small group is to provide a safe environment where that talking can take place. Unlike the family reunion, where after the ride home everyone remains scattered until next time, this family reunites. When the small groups have finished their time for discussion they all come back together for a recap as a large group once again.

There are dangers—occupational hazards, if you will—for the leaders of both the large group and the small group experiences. The first and greatest is the temptation to have the definitive answer, the final word, the great truth. Not only is it unnecessary for the leader to have all of the right answers, it's not very helpful. Even if you have all of the mysteries of the faith completely figured out (and good luck to you on that one!) the answers you give will not become the other person's answers until they have had a chance to think and talk and pray about them.

The second danger is that you'll allow this whole process to become dull, boring, repetitive, and, well, a whole lot like "church." Christians in general—and Lutherans in particular—have often been guilty of taking stimulating stuff, like the gospel and God's work in the world, and making it stuffy. Don't take yourself, this course, or any of the activities too seriously. Whether you "get it right" or not, the sun will still come up tomorrow (most likely). No one's eternal salvation rests on the outcome of this course. It is not a matter of life and death. There are life and death issues here, to be sure. But what we do with them doesn't decide the outcome. As soon as we start treating them seriously, it takes the fun right out of the conversation. The topics have enough weight in themselves, you don't need to add more pounds by getting all wound up about it.

So relax, have fun. Come to the reunion. Eat a little, sing a little, laugh a whole lot. Enjoy yourself and enjoy the company of those with whom you are gathering.

SETTING UP THE LUTHERAN COURSE

As the leader of The Lutheran Course, you are responsible for leading the large group portion of each session. This leader book will assist you with that task beginning with the next section, and continuing with the individual sessions that follow. But your leadership responsibilities also include some preliminary tasks before the course even starts. This section will outline those tasks for you.

Scheduling

As large group leader, you have the important task of coordinating the course. That is, you will need to gain support for the course among congregational leaders, establish a schedule of sessions, recruit key leaders, and then see to it that the course is announced and promoted to potential participants. It's not as difficult as it might appear. Just follow these steps.

Before doing anything else, consult with your pastor(s) and congregation council to make sure you have their support for conducting The Lutheran Course in your congregation. If you were recruited by the pastor for this duty, you can be pretty certain that you have the support to go ahead with the course. If you *are* the pastor, be sure to tell your education committee and/or your congregation council about the course. If applicable, also consult with your spouse. You know that Martin Luther would never commit to another evening a week away from home and family without consulting with Katie.

It will be necessary to determine the time frame available for each session when scheduling. The Lutheran Course ideally takes place in seven sessions over seven weeks, beginning each session with a meal and extending for a couple hours or more thereafter. But in some situations the ideal is not practical. More detailed information on planning how to use session time appears on page 18. But for now the concern is blocking out the necessary time. If the time for each session must be less than 90 minutes, you will need to double the number of sessions. Thus the seven-session course, if restricted to 45 minutes to an hour on Sunday mornings, will require 14 weeks.

You will set the time and place the course will occur. Consult your local listings to avoid scheduling the course on the same evening as your favorite television show. Be sure to also check your congregation's calendar of events to avoid conflicts and make sure the necessary space will be available. Assuming that you will be using all suggested segments for each session, you will need a place for the Table Talk and a place for the large group meeting. These might be the same space, such as a church fellowship hall with tables. Or, you may wish to move from the fellowship hall into the church nave, or to some other location where a video system is available, for the large group session. You'll also need a small room, such as a Sunday school room, for each of the small groups. Make sure all of these rooms will be available for each of the sessions. Don't forget to schedule an extra meeting time, just with the small group leaders, a week or so prior to the first session.

The Team

As the large group leader, you might want to recruit others to help with the course and make it relaxing and fun for everyone.

Publicist
This course will be pretty dull if there are no participants. So unless you want to sit home and watch the DVD by yourself, you'll need to do some recruiting. You will undoubtedly want participants to sign up in advance of the first session (though you probably don't want to turn away those procrastinators who don't make up their minds until the second session, either). With registration, you will be able to plan and establish the small group portion of the experience.

Follow these three easy steps to promote The Lutheran Course:

1. Be sure that you emphasize that the course is for life-long Lutherans, as well as for prospective members, when you speak or write about the course in your congregation.

2. Begin advertising The Lutheran Course to your potential audience at least a month in advance.

3. Use all available communication channels with the adults in your congregation (bulletins, newsletters, and verbal announcements during worship). Also use the bulletin inserts, posters, and the DVD commercial for the course, which are available in The Lutheran Course Promo Pack (ISBN 0-8066-5284-5).

Musician(s)
Recruit the best person, or the best ensemble, that you possibly can. Help them understand that you want the singing to be lively. Music suggestions are provided in this leader book for each session, and these are restricted to current Lutheran worship books. *LBW* refers to *Lutheran Book of Worship,* *WOV* refers to *With One Voice,* *RWS* refers to *Renewing Worship Songbook.* But the musicians should not feel restricted. If they have other appropriate music, turn them loose. Energy and a sense of humor are required in this job description.

Table Talk Coordinator
You probably know someone in your congregation who just loves to throw a good party. It may not have occurred to you before that this may be a spiritual gift. Though not listed as such in 1 Corinthians 12, a person with this gift is just what you need in charge of the Table Talk segment. Table Talk usually involves food—a whole meal if you can work that out, or at least dessert or snacks. It also involves an atmosphere of celebration, good conversation, and some surprises. There are suggestions for how to set up the Table Talk and get the conversation started for each session in this leader book. A truly gifted party person, who has some sensitivity for the theme and message of each session, can creatively launch from these suggestions.

Small Groups and Small Group Leaders
As participants sign up for the course, you will need to assign them to small groups of five to seven participants per group. Use your own judgment about how participants are placed in groups. While it is great to have a cross section of ages and situations, group members will be most comfortable if they share something in common with others in the group. The primary goal is to create groups in which members trust one another enough to share thoughts and feelings openly.

You'll also need to recruit one participant to serve as the leader for each of the small groups. This person does not need to be a theologically trained expert. Rather, the small group leader need only be someone self-confident enough, and gregarious enough, to start a conversation and invite others into it. Try to avoid appointing persons who will dominate or monopolize the conversation.

Avoid the temptation to make the small group larger so that you don't need to recruit as many small group leaders. When a small group isn't small anymore, the *small* group leader's job becomes much more difficult, and you will ensure the failure of the small groups, and therefore the failure of the whole course. Small groups must be small enough so that even shy people will feel comfortable speaking up. That won't happen in a group of ten or twenty. Because small group leaders don't need to be experts, it shouldn't be difficult to recruit one from among every six or seven who sign up to be participants.

Training

One thing that will help you recruit small group leaders is your promise to train them in all that they will need to know. This will mean setting up one meeting with them prior to the first session so that you can walk through the instructions with them. This meeting may be the only training they need. But many may feel better if they meet with you several times through the course, and a few may wish to meet prior to every session. You know your small group leaders best (after all, you recruited them), so determine how frequently you will need to spend time with them in preparation.

At the first meeting, you'll want to accomplish the following with the small group leaders:
- give them their copies of *The Lutheran Handbook* and help them become familiar with its purpose and tone
- give them their copies of the workbook for this course and explain what parts are used in large group and what parts are used in small group
- overview for them the shape of a typical session (see pp. 14–19)
- pass out copies of the Small Group Leader's Guide (pp. 99–100)
- show them a bit of the DVD, including the course overview segment with Martin and Katie
- pat them on the back, thank them often, and tell them what a great job they will do

Materials and Preparation
Finally, you will need to order a sufficient number of copies of *The Lutheran Handbook* and of *The Lutheran Course Workbook* for each participant so that they will arrive in time for the first session.

In addition to these preliminaries, you'll need to make sure that the space for the large group meeting is properly prepared prior to each session. More on these sorts of details will be found in the next section and in the individual sessions.

YOUR ROLE AS THE LARGE GROUP LEADER

As the large group leader and course coordinator, you should regard everything in this leader book and in the workbook as tools that are at your disposal. Generally, a worker does not feel compelled to use every tool in the toolbox just to have the satisfaction of saying the tools were all worth bringing along. Rather, the worker uses the right tool for the task at hand, and other tools will probably come in handy for other jobs on other days. Use what is here as you see fit, and ignore anything that is unnecessary or not helpful in your circumstances. You may also have some tools lying around that aren't in this particular toolbox, and you should certainly toss those in if you feel they will be helpful.

Table Talk

In this leader book, the informal sharing time that begins each session is called *Table Talk*, similar to the sort of conversation Martin and Katie Luther shared with their students and guests around the table at the old Augustinian cloister at Wittenberg. The Table Talk section for each session will suggest ways you can have the talking space prepared in order to get people thinking, talking, and having fun with things related to that session. Not all suggestions here will fit in your circumstances, but allow yourself to be creative and add your own touches. The reproducible pages on pages 102–110 will help you prepare Table Talk for each session.

The Table Talk period might take only ten minutes if you are just doing what is outlined for the session. If there is a potluck or other meal involved, it can take a half hour or more. If the eating is restricted to desserts only, you can compromise at twenty minutes. But don't ever rush dessert. Savor it as a gift of God. To truly get into the spirit of Martin and Katie's table talk would probably involve serving a dark Saxon ale, but please respect local customs.

Large Group Stuff

As the large group leader, you have primary responsibility for what takes place during the large group portion of each session. This doesn't mean that you do everything (you have and will recruit people to help), but it does mean that you serve as the host and that you will try to keep everything moving along and related to the central theme of each session. Each session in this leader book begins with an Overview paragraph. This paragraph is not meant to be read or shared in the large group, but is there to help you better understand that central theme and the points that will be brought up in other parts of the session.

The Opening

The part of the large group gathering that involves singing and preparation for the video is creatively referred to as the *Opening*. The Opening section will suggest some songs and hymns from worship books typically found in Lutheran churches these days. Recall that "A Mighty Fortress Is Our God" was set to a tune previously sung in pubs by college students until Luther turned it into a respectable hymn. Whoever is leading the songs should feel free to use whatever music he or she thinks will work best in your own situation. But the music should relate to the session theme in at least some way, even if it was previously sung in taverns.

Also included in the Opening will be suggestions for a scripture reading and for prayers. It's good to involve participants by selecting some to take turns with the readings and prayers. Or you, as the large group leader, may take on these tasks yourself if you feel that you really must. More than twenty minutes of Opening is probably overdoing it, but be sensitive to the mood of participants and vary accordingly.

The Introduction

Next comes the part where you, as the large group leader, will play your most important role. Your job is to set the stage for this presentation by introducing the speaker, topic, and video commercial. The Introduction section of this leader book will provide you with the information you will need. This information will appear in outline form, because it will be best if you can put it into your own words.

The Video

You should have the video presentation ready to go as soon as the introduction is concluded. Nothing stops the family reunion in its tracks more abruptly than having problems with the video equipment. So please set everything up before participants begin to arrive and test everything to make sure it will work properly at the right moment.

You might want to bring even more humor to the course with the commercial skits on the Video Commercials DVD. These skits are edgy, funny, and even a bit irreverent, yet intended for new Lutherans, old Lutherans, and anyone in between. One "commercial" is provided for each session in this course.

It's important for the screen to be large enough for everyone to see, but even more important is that the sound be loud enough and clear enough for all to hear and understand the speaker. The presentations generally last just over 15 minutes. (Pages 63–98 of this leader book contain transcripts of the video presentations. Use these reference materials as needed.) When the presentation is done, show the video commercial for the session.

The Workbook

After the video it's time to turn attention to the workbook. In most cases you will have directed participants to the proper pages as part of your introduction to the video. Directions for this portion vary from session to session, but should always be done fairly quickly—within five to ten minutes. There are four workbook pages for each session. Two pages of the workbook for each session, called Large Group Stuff, are designed for use during or after the video in the large group. The purpose of these workbook pages is to reinforce the main points of the video, and to give those who really need to raise their hands in the large group the opportunity to let others know that they got the right answers. Pick and choose among the exercises offered in the workbook, selecting one or two that will help reinforce the points made by the video. It is not necessary to review everything or to complete every exercise in the Large Group Stuff pages of the workbook. Move through this and let the less assertive participants get on to the small groups where they will feel more comfortable talking. In the small groups they will continue with the two additional workbook pages, called Small Group Stuff, that are designed for use in generating small group discussion.

If you are conducting The Lutheran Course on Sunday mornings, or in some other limited time frame in which you are splitting each session over two weeks, plan on ending with these workbook pages when wrapping up the first half of the session, and beginning with them again the following week as a review. Some of the exercises in the Large Group Stuff pages may be used immediately after the video, and others may be used for review the next time before they go to their small groups. Table 1 (p. 18) offers some suggested time frames for use of the material.

There's probably time for at least one more song before the whole gang breaks up and heads off to their small groups (or home until next time, if you are working with limited time).

Small Group Stuff

While participants are busy conversing in their small groups, you as large group leader should take a break. You've earned it by working hard up to now. Above all, resist the temptation to go barging into small groups to hear what they are saying. Many Lutherans, particularly clergy, will feel guilty about not being productive during this period. Sit back and let the Spirit work. If you simply cannot relax and do nothing during this time, read from Martin Luther's Basic Theological Writings until the small group time is over and participants come back for the Wrap-up.

Wrap-up

In Luke 10:17 we read, "The seventy returned with joy, saying, 'Lord, in your name even the demons submit to us!'" The Wrap-up time will have a similar atmosphere. Caution the participants against violating any confidences before calling on anyone. Allow a few small groups to report on any insights they gained or entertain any questions they may have raised. If the groups are quiet (unlikely), ask about a specific Small Group Stuff question, or return to the Large Group Stuff pages of the workbook. And yes, there's always time for one more song.

Usually, it will be suggested that a reading assignment be made as part of the Wrap-up time. This reading from *The Lutheran Handbook* will lead into the next session. There will also be other references to *The Lutheran Handbook* along the way.

Table 1. Session planning guide

Total session length	Table Talk	Opening	Intro & Video	Workbook	Small Group Stuff	Wrap-up
2 ½ hours	40 min.	20 min.	20 min.	10 min.	50 min.	10 min.
2 hours*	30 min.	15 min.	20 min.	5 min.	40 min.	10 min.
1 ½ hours	15 min.	10 min.	20 min.	5 min.	35 min.	5 min.
1 hour (week one)	15 min.	15 min.	20 min.	10 min.	skip until next time	
1 hour (week two)	pick up from the previous time			10 min.	40 min.	10 min.
45 minutes (week one)	5 min.	10 min.	20 min.	10 min.	skip until next time	
45 minutes (week two)	pick up from the previous time			5 min.	35 min.	5 min.

*The ideal session length would be at least two hours

Summary of Each Session
(Experiment. See what works best in *your* situation.)

Table Talk
Ideas and discussion starters to use as participants arrive.

Large Group Stuff
Opening: Music, scripture reading, and prayer suggestions for use in the large group gathering.
Introduction: Introduction to the video presentation and commercial.
Video: Viewing of the video presentation.
Workbook: Large Group Stuff pages of the workbook to reinforce the video.

Small Group Stuff
Small Group Stuff pages of the workbook to generate discussion.

Wrap-up
Brief closing time.

Evaluation

At the end of Session 7, be sure to have participants fill out the Course Evaluation Form (p. 110). Review this feedback to find out what went well and what could be improved. Then consider offering the course again. Some of those who just finished the course might be willing and available to help with this.

HOW TO TELL THE DIFFERENCE BETWEEN THE LAW AND THE GOSPEL

Overview *(background and orientation just for you as the leader)*

If you've ever had to learn a foreign language, especially as an adult, you know that it can be tough going. The Lutheran Course begins with a grammar lesson in speaking Lutheran. The vocabulary list only includes a few words like "law" and "gospel." You don't have to learn to say, "Where is the bathroom, please?" in Lutheran. In this session's video presentation, James Nestingen speaks about Christ Jesus as the subject of the verbs. It's all about learning a new way of speaking. Because those who know they are both sinners and saints have completely different ways of describing themselves, the world, and their relationship with God, it means learning a new vocabulary. Nestingen uses the Latin phrase, *opinio legis*, to describe the insidious way in which the law continues to create doubt in our hearts through "if-then" vocabulary. *If* I offer God a life of good deeds (or at least good intentions), *then* I'll be given God's blessing in return. By contrast, the gospel uses "because-therefore" vocabulary. *Because* Christ has died for the ungodly, *therefore* the sinner (that is, you and I) can hope for redemption. The cross is the prior condition. Upon the cross all salvation rests, through it all hope arises, and because of it all truly good works are done. Nestingen goes on to suggest two uses for the law: to keep order in the world, and to drive our consciences toward the gospel.

The law continues to create doubt in our hearts through "if-then" vocabulary . . .
The gospel uses "because-therefore" vocabulary.

Preparation

Objective: Each participant will understand the Lutheran distinction between law and gospel, and the Lutheran proposal to view the gospel through the lens of grace as a gift.

Materials needed: anything necessary for singing (instruments, songbooks, etc.), copies of the Table Talk questions for Session 1 (p. 102), copies of the Session 1 handout (p. 101), and a copy of *The Lutheran Handbook* and *The Lutheran Course Workbook* for each participant.

Prepare yourself for the session: Read through all the Session 1 material in this leader book and the workbook. Also view the Session 1 video presentation and commercial in advance.

Prepare the room: Have the video presentation set up, make sure everything works, that it is properly cued and ready to play. Also have the Video Commercials DVD on hand.

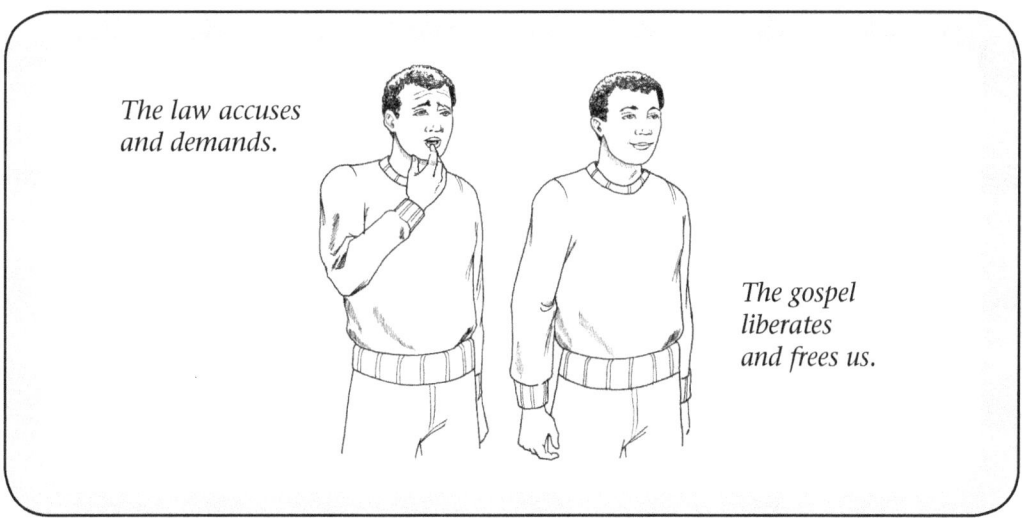

Table Talk

Because this is the first session, plan on having stick-on or pin-on name tags available as participants arrive.

Participants will be discussing these questions:

- When you hear the word, "Lutheran," what's the first thing that comes to mind?
- What's the funniest story you've ever heard about someone getting pulled over by the police while driving?
- Have you ever been called to jury duty? If so, what was it like?
- If you weren't here at this gathering, where would you be and what would you be doing right now?

You will need to have a set of four Table Talk cards laying face down on each table where participants will sit as they gather or eat. To make the cards, photocopy page 102 and cut on the dotted lines.

Suggest that one person pick up a card at random, provide an answer, and pass it to the person to their right, who will also answer and pass the card on. When that card has gone around the table, someone else can pick up another and repeat the process until the time is up.

Large Group Stuff

Opening
Begin with some instrumental music as people are gathering. At the appointed beginning time, have the group sing something lively, then sing something livelier still, then begin to settle into a more mellow mood. Some suggestions for this session are *With One Voice* (WOV) 791, 744, 612, 717, 731.

Have a brief reading from scripture. Suggestion for this session: Romans 5:1-11.

Pray. Participants may be invited to offer petitions. Conclude with your own prayer thanking God for the gift of the gospel of Christ.

Session 1

Introduction
Briefly introduce the video presenter as James A. Nestingen, Professor of Church History at Luther Seminary in St. Paul, Minnesota, where he has taught for over a quarter century. Nestingen has many published works and lectures on Luther's catechisms and confessional Lutheran theology. His books include *Manger in the Mountains* (1999); *The Faith We Hold* (1983); *Martin Luther: His Life and His Writings* (1982); *Roots of Our Faith* (1978); and *Free to Be* (with Gerhard Forde, 1975).

Point out question 1 in the Large Group Stuff in the workbook (p. 8) and prepare participants to follow along.

Explain that James Nestingen will introduce a Latin phrase, *opinio legis,* which might literally be translated as, "speculation about the law." He uses this term to draw a distinction between the law and the gospel.

According to Nestingen, Lutherans propose to see all of the Bible through the lens of the gospel. The gospel always begins with what God has done for us. The *opinio legis* always tries to draw us back to what we must do for God. The "speculation" is always about the question, "Have I done enough?" The answer to that question is always, "No." But God in Christ has done everything.

And now a word from our sponsor: In this session's video commercial, long-suffering "Katie Lu" is having trouble removing stains from her husband's shirt. Find out how Martin "Winkie" Luther saves the day with Law and Gospel, a laundry spray and detergent.

Video
Play the video presentation. Then play the commercial for "Law & Gospel brand laundry detergent."

Workbook
Point out that the first two workbook pages in each session are for Large Group Stuff (large group use), and the next two pages in each session are for Small Group Stuff (small group use).

Ask if there are any initial questions or reactions to the video presentation and commercial (see p. 24).

❶ Ask for volunteers to share what they wrote in the blanks for question 1. There are *no wrong answers* to this question, but what the authors had in mind would be something like this:

Leader Book 23

- "Justification by faith" is *Christ's work, a free gift, etc.*
- Law is an *if-then* proposition, gospel is a *because-therefore* fact.
- The *opinio legis* is a false belief that *the Law will set everything right, etc.*
- The same Word of God can function as both law and gospel, depending upon *the way one hears, one's need at the moment, one's conscience, the opinio legis, etc.*

❷ Distribute copies of the Session 1 handout (p. 101). This question follows directly on the end of question 1, above. Point out that in the first scripture passage, there is a command ("Go!") and there are also promises ("I will bless you . . ."). One way to read this passage is "if-then": *If* you go, *then* I will bless you. But another way to read the passage is "because-therefore": *Because* Abram and Sarai trust the promises, *therefore* they are set free to go on a journey to an unknown land.

Go through the other scriptures, but let participants suggest ways each might be read as "if-then" or "because-therefore." Do not make people choose which reading they prefer, just help them to see the difference in interpretation of each passage. You do not need to go through all of these passages, just enough for participants to grasp the concept. If you are splitting the session between two time periods, such as Sunday mornings, be sure to save several of these scripture texts to use as review at the beginning of the next time together.

❸ Ask volunteers for responses. One way to state this is that the law makes us aware of our sin and the gospel sets us free. "Winkie" is careful to point out that neither product works alone, but the combination does the trick.

Conclude Large Group Stuff with another song or two. Suggestions: *WOV* 715, 724.

As seen in the video commercial, Law & Gospel brand laundry detergent gets out today's tough stains with the dual action of God's Word.

Small Group Stuff

Dismiss the groups for Small Group Stuff (the "ride home" portion of the session in small groups) and let them know what time to return for Wrap-up. Relax.

Wrap-up

After the small groups return, remind participants not to violate any confidences in talking about their small group time together with the larger group.

Ask participants what insights they gained into the Lutheran language of "law" and "gospel" as they talked in their small groups. What questions do they still have?

It is quite possible that some will be insistent that "there is no free lunch" and that God demands certain things from us in order that we might be saved. Don't be too aggressive in challenging this view. Simply ask these participants to try to keep their minds open as this concept continues to be worked out in the rest of the course.

Be sure to announce the reading for the next session: *The Lutheran Handbook*, pages 52–61 and 131–133. (Of course, participants can read more of the Handbook if they get started and can't stop!)

Suggestion for a closing song: *WOV 699*.

FIVE THINGS YOU SHOULD KNOW ABOUT THE LUTHERAN REFORMATION

Overview *(background and orientation just for you as the leader)*

The world Martin Luther was born into in 1483 was a world unlike the one we know. As Ken Sundet Jones says in the video presentation, life was "nasty, brutish, and short." Because of the plague and countless other diseases, one could expect to see death on a regular basis. There was little distinction between the government and the Catholic Church, and Rome had a hand in practically every stage of a person's life. By the time Luther lay in his deathbed in Eisleben in 1546, the world had changed. The number of sacraments, for Luther's followers, had been reduced to two. Religious activities had been completely reinterpreted. The church itself had been split in two (with more splits to come). The modern notion of a nation state had begun to rise. And although death remained a constant (and still does), there came a new way of thinking about both our lives now and God's gift of eternal life in Christ when we die.

Luther was a brilliant but troubled young man who became a monk out of fear of God's wrath. As Luther struggled with his own faith, he was called on by his monastic order to teach the Bible at the new University of Wittenberg. He experienced the same kinds of pressures we all do, as he busied himself with teaching, preaching, writing, and administrative affairs. Somehow, in the midst of all of that, Luther came to see scripture in a different light. That realization has come to be known as Luther's theological breakthrough. He tested this new idea by reading the Bible under those terms: God knows sinners

God knows sinners can't climb a religious ladder of righteousness; God instead comes to us with love and mercy in Jesus Christ.

can't climb a religious ladder of righteousness; God instead comes to us with love and mercy in Jesus Christ. Luther's way of thinking about the Bible, Jesus, the sacraments, and evangelism was shaped by his conviction that there's nothing you can do to get to God. That's how Luther arrived at the law and gospel thinking that runs through each session in The Lutheran Course. This thinking is summarized in Luther's last written words, discovered shortly after his death: "We are beggars. This is true."

Preparation

Objective: Each participant will understand that Martin Luther was a sixteenth-century Catholic priest who sought to reform his church, but who was expelled from it for his understanding of law and gospel.

Materials needed: anything necessary for singing (instruments, songbooks, etc.), copies of "The 9.5 Theses" (p. 103) for Table Talk, a copy of *The Lutheran Handbook* and workbook for each participant.

Prepare yourself for the session: Read through all the Session 2 material in this leader book and the workbook. Also view the video presentation and commercial in advance.

Prepare the room: Have the video presentation set up, make sure everything works, that it is properly cued, and ready to play. Also have the Video Commercials DVD on hand.

Table Talk

Place a copy of "The 9.5 Theses" on each table and invite participants to discuss it as they gather and eat.

Large Group Stuff

Opening
Begin with some instrumental music as people are gathering. At the appointed beginning time, have the group sing something lively, then livelier still, then begin to settle into a more mellow mood. Some suggestions for this session are *LBW* 14, 390, 393, and 229.

Have a brief reading from scripture. Suggestion for this session: Ephesians 2:4-10.

Pray. Participants may be invited to offer petitions. Conclude with your own prayer thanking God for the gift of the gospel of Christ.

Introduction
Briefly introduce the video presenter as Ken Sundet Jones, Assistant Professor of Philosophy and Religion at Grand View College in Des Moines, Iowa. He is one of the contributing writers to *The Lutheran Handbook* and Here We Stand, a new confirmation curriculum. Point out question 1 in Large Group Stuff in the workbook (p. 12) and prepare participants to follow along.

Explain that an *indulgence* was a written certificate guaranteeing forgiveness of sins to the person who purchased it from a specially appointed priest. Money from the sale was being used to build St. Peter's Basilica in Rome, and many poor peasants were being made to feel that the only way to obtain salvation for themselves and their loved ones was through such a purchase. Note that Luther was an unlikely champion for the gospel because he had struggled with it so much in his life. Point out that Luther's goal was not to form a new church, or even to leave his vows as a monk and priest. Rather, as a loyal Catholic, he wanted to end a practice that he saw as an abuse of people and a perversion of the gospel.

And now a word from our sponsor: In this session's video commercial, we see Martin "Winkie" Luther laboring over one his many writings. The real Martin Luther, who lived some 500 years ago, was a prolific writer of tracts, pamphlets, and books about church doctrine and theology. Unlike reformers and theologians before him, Luther benefited from a new technology, the movable-type printing press, invented by fellow German Johannes Gutenburg just a few decades prior to Luther's birth.

Video
Play the video presentation. Then play the commercial for the "Gutenberg fax-copier-printer."

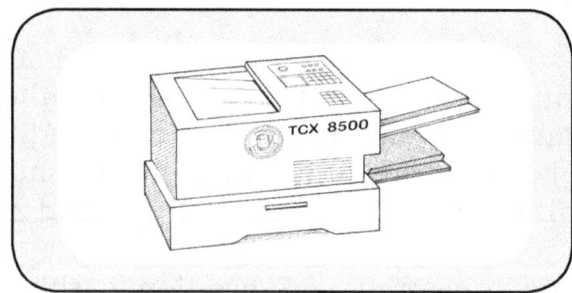

As seen in the video commercial, the breakthrough laser quill technology of the Gutenberg fax-copier-printer is the best thing to happen to reformers like Martin Luther since movable type.

Session 2

Workbook
Note: The first two workbook pages in each session are for Large Group Stuff (large group use), and the next two pages in each session are for Small Group Stuff (small group use).

❶ Ask if there are any initial questions or reactions to the video presentation and commercial (see p. 28). Ask for volunteers to share what they wrote in the blanks in the workbook. *There are no wrong answers* to these questions, but what the authors had in mind would be something like this:
- In Luther's day, life was *nasty, brutish, and short, etc.*
- As a monk, young Martin Luther *was avid, scrupulous, went whole hog, etc.*
- After Luther was appointed to be a Bible professor *he discovered the gospel, things made sense, he found clarity, etc.*
- Because of the newly invented printing press, *Luther's Theses became "flying letters."*
- At Luther's death he made it clear *we are beggars, life is repenting again and again, etc.*
- What other main point(s) did you hear? *Responses will vary.*

❷ "The joyful exchange" lists have a number of possible right answers, such as:

When you are joined to Christ (by grace through faith)	
Jesus gives you his:	in exchange for your:
righteousness	*culpability*
innocence	guilt
blessedness	*cursedness*
obedience	rebellion
purity	*muck*
commendation	condemnation
life	*death*

Leader Book 29

❸ Based on his study of the Bible, Luther believed that some of the practices of the church in his day needed to change. Another way to state the question would be: What kind of circumstances would cause us to take a stand against the church or religious practices today? Answers might include a conviction that the current situation is wrong, harmful to faith, or inconsistent with the Bible. Point out that Luther may not have known the impact he would have, but he certainly was someone with strong convictions and a life centered on Christ.

Conclude with another song or two. Suggestions: *LBW* 230, 239.

Small Group Stuff

Dismiss the groups for Small Group Stuff (the "ride home" portion of the session in small groups) and let them know what time to return for Wrap-up. Relax.

Lutherans and non-Lutherans alike credit Martin Luther (1483-1546) for spearheading the Reformation by raising important questions about the church and translating the church and translating the Bible for everyday people.

Wrap-up

After the small groups return, remind participants not to violate any confidences in talking about their small group time together with the larger group.

Ask participants what insights they gained into Luther and the Reformation as they talked in their small groups. What questions do they still have?

It is quite possible that some will still be confused about Luther's place in history. History is abstract and difficult for some to grasp. Dates and chronologies are not important (other than knowing that Dr. Martin Luther and Dr. Martin Luther King, Jr. were different people in different centuries). Focus on Luther's understanding of the gospel and his courage in facing personal danger to proclaim it.

Be sure to announce the reading for the next session: *The Lutheran Handbook*, pages 34–35 and 214–216.

Suggestion for a closing song: *LBW* 260.

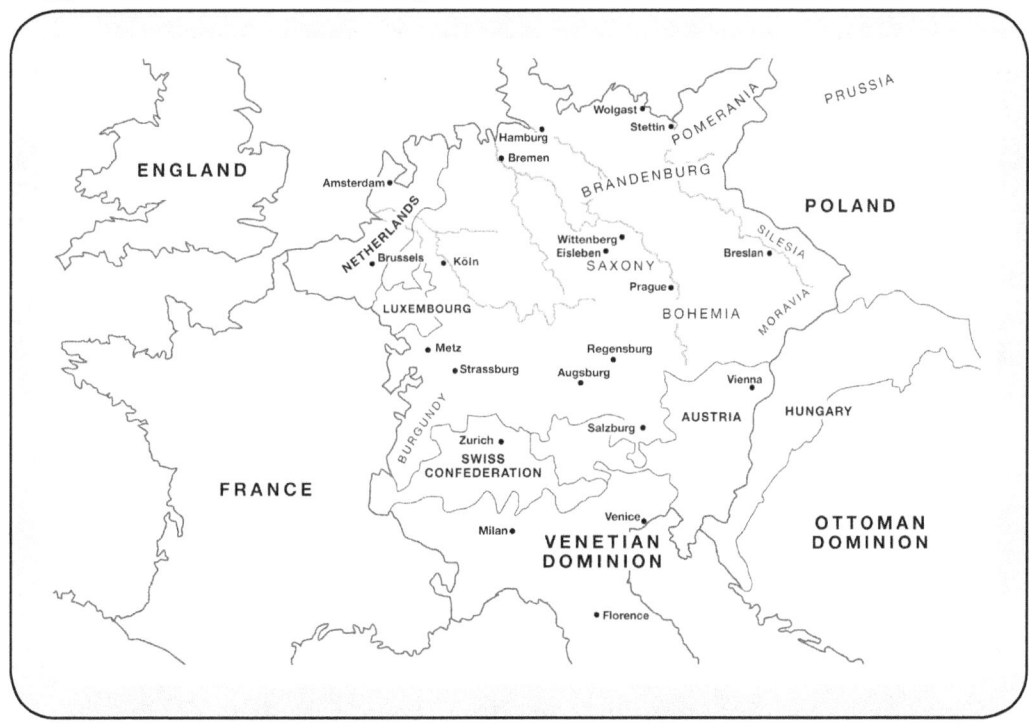

Martin Luther was born in the town of Eisleben on November 10, 1483. He received his doctor of theology degree from the University of Wittenberg, where he taught from 1508 to 1546. In 1530, the Lutheran reformers traveled to the city of Augsburg to defend their teachings. Luther died in Eisleben on February 18, 1546.

THE ANATOMY OF A BAPTISM

Overview *(background and orientation just for you as the leader)*

A sacrament is a means by which God's transcendent presence and loving grace become tangible for humans living in a physical world. Luther defined sacraments more narrowly than his predecessors in the church. His goal was to safeguard the free gift that comes from God and to make sure the sacraments were instituted by God and not by human beings. Thus, a rite had to have three parts for it to be a sacrament. First, it had to be commanded of believers by Jesus. Second, it had to involve a created element. Finally, it had to convey the promise of God for the ungodly. When Luther applied these criteria, just two sacraments remained: baptism and the Lord's Supper.

The water of baptism is put together with a word of promise in such a way that God's eternal will for faith and life happens. God pours the baptismal waters to wash sin away. Some Christians baptize babies, others only adults. But to dwell on the question of age is to miss one of the most important implications of the sacrament: baptism is for sinners. In Romans 3:23, Paul tells us that "all have sinned and fall short of the glory of God." If that's so (and it is), then everyone is in dire need of this powerful combination of ordinary water and the extraordinary divine Word: seven-month-olds, seven-year-olds, and seventy-year-olds. In any case, baptism isn't some sort of insurance policy that guarantees heaven when we die. Lutherans do not baptize babies in case they die. Rather, Lutherans baptize people in case they live. It is a guarantee of God's presence to sustain us and strengthen us

> *Baptism allows you to be true to your twin identities: sinner and saint. Thus the Christian life is one of constant repentance for sin and constant claiming of God's baptismal promise.*

every day, here and now—and forever is an added bonus. Some insist on hard evidence that the person being baptized will, in fact, continue his or her life in faith. But no one has a crystal ball that allows peering into the future. And even if we could see the future, the real issue is not what the baptized person does but what God does in baptism. If we think the aim of baptism is to create morally upright people, we'll be disappointed. Baptism allows you to be true to your twin identities: sinner and saint. Thus the Christian life is one of constant repentance for sin and constant claiming of God's baptismal promise.

Preparation

Objective: Each participant will understand that baptism is a sacrament of belonging to God's family, and an act of God for each of us in which God bestows promises that strengthen us for daily living.

Materials needed: anything necessary for singing (instruments, songbooks, etc.), water toys, copies of the Table Talk questions for Session 3 (p. 104), something to award as a small prize for correct answers to the matching exercise in the Large Group Stuff segment of the workbook, and a copy of *The Lutheran Handbook* and workbook for each participant.

Prepare yourself for the session: Read through all the Session 3 material in this leader book and the workbook. Also view the video presentation and commercial in advance.

Prepare the room: Have the video presentation set up, make sure everything works, that it is properly cued, and ready to play. Also have the Video Commercials DVD on hand.

Table Talk

Have bowls of water on the tables when the group gathers. Or, if possible (in the spirit of Winking Luther), consider putting a child's wading pool in the middle of the room (with water in it, of course). Also consider the possibility of providing squirt guns or (for the truly daring) water balloons for participants.

Photocopy page 104. Lay a set of cards face down on each table where participants will sit as they gather or eat. Suggest that one person pick up a card at random, provide an answer, and pass it to the person to their right, who will also answer and pass it on. When that card has gone around the table, someone else can pick up another and repeat the process until the time is up.

- What's the most fun you've ever had with water?
- When have you been frightened by water?
- Relate an experience you've had with wind and water together.
- What is the most beautiful watery place you've ever seen?

Large Group Stuff

Opening
Begin with some instrumental music as people are gathering. At the appointed beginning time, have the group sing something lively, then livelier still, then begin to settle into a more mellow mood. Some suggestions for this session are *RWS* R290, R164, R159, and R163.

Have two brief readings from scripture. Suggestion for this session: John 4:7-14 and Titus 3:3-7.

Pray. Participants may be invited to offer petitions. Conclude with your own prayer thanking God for the gift of the gospel of Christ.

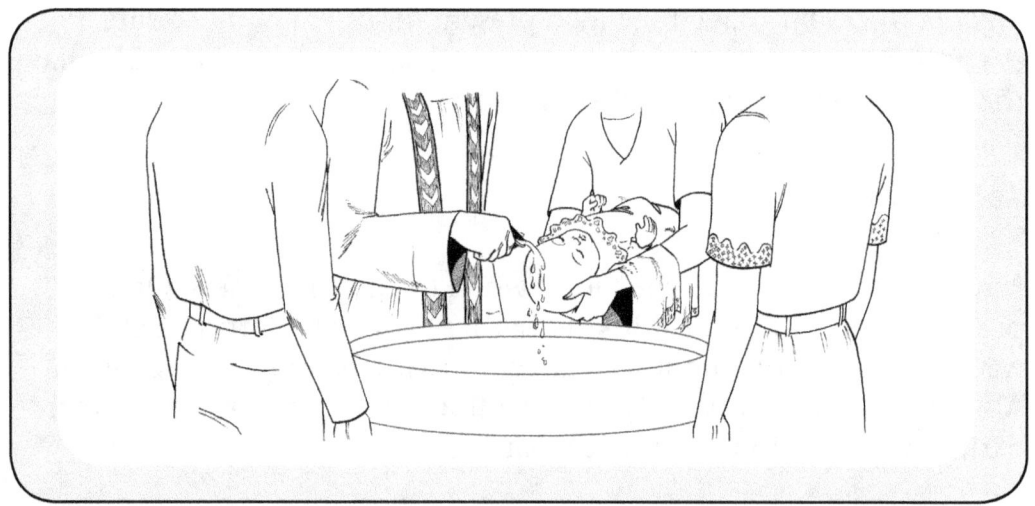

God is the true actor in baptism, bringing everyone involved to the font and inspiring trust and faith. Note: Lutherans baptize people of all ages—not just infants.

Introduction
Briefly introduce the video presenter as Winston Persaud, a native of Guyana, South America, and now Professor of Systematic Theology at Wartburg Theological Seminary in Dubuque, Iowa. Persaud, a well-known author, is in great demand as a speaker both nationally and globally.

Point out question 1 in Large Group Stuff in the workbook (p. 16) and prepare participants to follow along. (Note that the first two workbook pages are for use in the large group, and the next two are for discussion in the small groups.)

Explain that Persaud will begin rather quickly with a definition of a sacrament, according to Luther's understanding, and that he will note in his initial remarks how baptism fits this understanding.

Point out that *The Lutheran Handbook* doesn't devote very many pages to baptism, aside from the two-page "Anatomy" on pages 34 and 35. This is a lot like the Bible. We never find in the New Testament any comprehensive argument about why we should baptize, how we should baptize, or whom we should baptize. Instead, the Bible writers, such as the apostle Paul and the writers of the gospels, assume all Christians are baptized and that they know quite a bit about baptism. They instruct us about the Christian life with baptism as a starting point, but never feel they have to make a case for baptism itself. So Lutherans also assume that baptism is a foundation for faith and life.

And now a word from our sponsor: "Katie Lu" and Martin "Winkie" Luther find themselves walking through puddles of water in a church. "Winkie" has been so carried away with baptism that he splashed water everywhere! Fortunately (and as usual) Katie has an answer to the problem.

Video
Play the video presentation. Then play the commercial for "Splashy Font brand baptismal napkins."

Workbook

Ask if there are any initial questions or reactions to the video presentation or commercial (see p. 37).

❶ Ask for volunteers to share what they wrote in the blanks in the workbook. *There are no wrong answers* to these questions, but what the authors had in mind would be something like this:

- For Lutheran Christians, baptism is *a summary of the Gospel.*
- It is absolutely essential to keep two things together: *water* and *word*.
- Baptism is not about *what we do*, but about *what God does in Christ.*
- Baptism is a *communal, public* event.
- Because of baptism we *live out the promise each day*.
- God's grace is *abundant, extravagant, etc.*
- What other main point(s) did you hear? *Answers will vary.*

❷ Give participants a few minutes to work on the matching exercise individually. The answers are:

C (Jesus, the Lord)
D (The apostle Paul)
B (Simon Peter)
A (John the Baptist, talking about Jesus).

Consider giving a small prize (such as a squirt gun) to those who have all the answers correct.

❸ "Winkie" says that the baptismal waters are physical and fun, perfect for washing sinners in God's amazing grace. His lavish use of the water might tell us that God's grace is lavish, abundant, and extravagant, too.

Conclude Large Group Stuff with another song or two. Suggestions: *RWS* R160, R161.

Small Group Stuff

Dismiss the groups for Small Group Stuff (the "ride home" portion of the session in small groups) and let them know what time to return for Wrap-up. Relax.

Session 3

Wrap-up

Remind participants not to violate any confidences in talking about their small group time together with the larger group.

Ask participants what they have learned from the discussion. What questions do they still have?

It is quite possible that some will still be questioning the concept of infant baptism. Hear those concerns. Note that various Christian traditions have always felt the need to mark critical life events—birth and acceptance into the community, coming of age in adolescence, marriage, death, etc. This need is the reason infant dedication is practiced by traditions that do not baptize infants, and the need for adult education and decision are also the reason for the Lutheran emphasis on the Rite of Affirmation of Baptism, or "confirmation." But beyond the mere social ceremony, Lutherans believe that the essential character of baptism is God's act of grace personalized for each one of us.

Be sure to announce the reading for the next session: *The Lutheran Handbook*, pages 36–40 and 222–223.

Suggestion for a closing song: R187 or R300 from *RWS*.

As seen in the video commercial, Splashy Font brand baptismal napkins come in handy when baptismal waters overflow.

Leader Book 37

HOW TO RECEIVE COMMUNION

Overview *(background and orientation just for you as the leader)*

Just as baptism meets Luther's definition of a sacrament, so, too, does the Lord's Supper: it is commanded by Christ in the gospels. Communion uses the created elements of bread and wine. And it is connected to God's Word in a way that brings faith to sinners. Where baptism is the sacrament of belonging that raises sinners to new life, the Lord's Supper is the sacrament in which God nourishes and sustains that life. This meal is a reminder that mealtimes are hallowed, for our daily bread (both the food we eat and the fellowship we share) is a gracious gift from God.

Jesus and the disciples were in Jerusalem for the annual Passover festival. It was during that meal that Jesus took some of the food and changed it from a meal about the past into one that blessed its eaters with a future. This sacrament goes by a number of different names: The Lord's Supper, Eucharist, Sacrament of the Altar, Holy Communion, etc. Each name emphasizes a different aspect of the sacrament. The details of what kind of bread and wine to use, and the mechanics of how they are distributed, should not distract from the central message. Lutherans say the bread and wine aren't mere symbols because Jesus promised to be there in them. Neither are the bread and wine turned into something else. Instead we talk about Jesus' "real presence" in the sacrament. Just *how* Christ is present is the mystery of God's incarnation in body and blood in the world in Jesus. There are some who think one must be especially worthy to receive Christ in this way. But that's not the way Lutherans have treated the

Where baptism is the sacrament of belonging that raises sinners to new life, the Lord's Supper is the sacrament in which God nourishes and sustains that life.

38   The Lutheran Course

sacrament. The best way we can receive the sacrament is to come to the altar—to use Luther's words—as a beggar. We bring nothing other than simple trust in Christ's promise to be present "for you"—that is, for each of us personally, as well as for the gathered community—for the forgiveness of sins, life here and now, and salvation forever.

Preparation

Objective: Each participant will understand the Lord's Supper as a gift of God's presence to nourish and sustain our faith by giving us exactly what is promised: forgiveness of sin, life, and salvation, regardless of our worthiness to receive these gifts.

Materials needed: anything necessary for singing (instruments, songbooks, etc.), bread baskets, other food and drink, copies of the Table Talk questions for Session 4 (p. 105), a copy of *The Lutheran Handbook* and workbook for each participant. You may wish to have some of your congregation's communion ware set up in the large group meeting area as visual aids.

Prepare yourself for the session: Read through all the Session 4 material in this leader book and the workbook. Also view the video presentation and commercial in advance.

Prepare the room: Have the video presentation set up, make sure everything works, that it is properly cued, and ready to play. Also have the Video Commercials DVD on hand.

Table Talk

Even if you haven't been involving food in your Table Talk time in other sessions, it would be particularly appropriate to do so for this session. In addition to the usual potluck meal or dessert, try to arrange to have a basket or tray of various breads on each table when participants arrive. Optional: If local customs, congregational regulations, and insurance regulations permit (consult with your pastor and congregation council) you might also consider placing a bottle of wine and glasses on each table, so that participants are sharing bread and a glass of wine as they eat together.

By this time, participants may begin, just naturally, to sit with other members of their small groups as they gather at Table Talk. If this hasn't happened already, you might suggest they do so at this session, so that each small group is seated at its own table.

Photocopy page 105 and place a set of cards at each table. Invite participants to discuss these questions as they are eating.

- What does the smell of fresh-baked bread bring to your mind? What is your best memory of bread or bread baking?
- What meal traditions are special to your family? Thanksgiving? Christmas? Family reunions? What special meals does your family eat together?
- Do you remember your "first communion"? How old were you? Who came to share the event with you? What other special events took place at that time? How did you feel about it?
- What was, for you, the most meaningful celebration of the Lord's Supper that you recall?

Large Group Stuff

Opening
Begin with instrumental music as people are gathering. At the appointed beginning time, have the group sing something lively, then livelier still, then begin to settle into a more mellow mood. Some suggestions for this session are *WOV* 719, 789, 705, 748, 717, 731.

Have a brief reading from scripture. Suggestion for this session: Luke 22:7-20.

Pray. Participants may be invited to offer petitions. Conclude with your own prayer thanking God for the gift of the gospel of Christ.

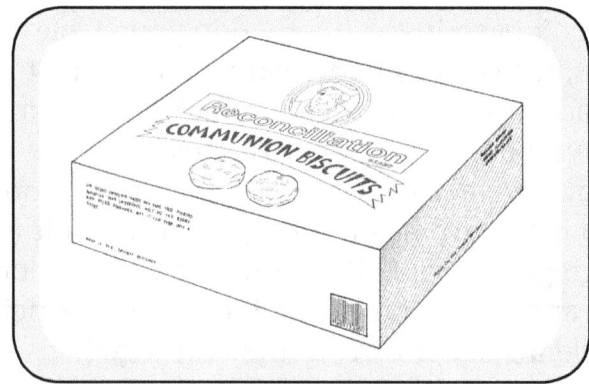

As seen in the video commercial, Reconciliation brand communion biscuits bring sinners together in Christ.

Session 4

Introduction

Briefly introduce the video presenter. Foster R. McCurley currently serves as Theologian-in-Residence for LUTHERCARE and Lutheran Social Services of South Central Pennsylvania—a position he took after retiring from twenty-five years as a seminary professor. During his academic career at Lutheran Theological Seminary at Philadelphia, McCurley served as Dean Professor of Old Testament and Hebrew. He is the author of eighteen books. Point out question 1 in the Large Group Stuff in the workbook (p. 20) and prepare participants to follow along.

Explain that Foster McCurley begins by responding to the question, "Why are there so many different names for this sacrament?" Participants will want to listen closely to his response. In fact, most of McCurley's presentation is a discussion of vocabulary—finding the right words to describe what goes on at the Lord's table.

According to McCurley, Lutherans have a unique perspective on the Lord's Supper that sets them apart both from Roman Catholics and from other Protestants. McCurley repeatedly downplays concerns about specific practices and keeps coming back to that central unique perspective. Listen carefully to hear what that perspective is.

And now a word from our sponsor: In this session's video commercial, "Katie Lu" is busy baking the "reconciliation biscuits" for the Lord's Supper. She is working so hard that one can hardly blame her for being short-tempered when her husband, Martin "Winkie" Luther, comes in asking stupid questions.

Video

Play the video presentation. Then play the commercial for "Reconciliation biscuits."

Workbook

Note: The first two workbook pages in each session are for Large Group Stuff (large group use), and the next two pages in each session are for Small Group Stuff (small group use).

Ask if there are any initial questions or reactions to the video presentation and commercial (see p. 40).

❶ Ask participants if they think they heard the unique Lutheran perspective on the sacrament that McCurley was emphasizing. *There are no wrong answers* for this question, but studying the transcript

Leader Book 41

in the back of this leader book will reveal that McCurley continues to emphasize Christ's promise to be truly present, while stepping away from particulars about the "stuff"—wine vs. grape juice, pastors vs. lay distributors, consuming vs. disposing of leftovers, etc. Christ comes to us as he has promised, *with* the eating and drinking. He comes not with magic stuff, but with ordinary stuff.

Ask for volunteers to share what they wrote in the blanks in the workbook. *There are no wrong answers* for these questions, but what the authors had in mind would be something like this:

- In the Lord's Supper the church proclaims *the Lord's death until he comes, future salvation, etc.*
- The best way to receive the sacrament is by *recognizing it as God's act, as beggars, etc.*
- The important words in the sacrament are, *"given and shed FOR YOU."*
- The bread and wine are *signs, more than symbols, they remain bread and wine, etc.*
- What you get in the Lord's Supper is *God's Word, forgiveness, new life, etc.*
- What other main point(s) did you hear? *Answers will vary.*

❷ Encourage participants to identify the similarities and differences in these accounts. Similarities include *in all accounts except John there is a loaf of bread and a cup, Jesus gives thanks or blesses the bread, Jesus says the bread and wine are his body and his blood, and there is a covenant; 1 Corinthians and Luke have the words "Do this, in remembrance of me." Matthew and Mark are the most similar.* Differences include: *1 Corinthians says this happened "on the night when he was betrayed;" in Luke, Jesus says he will not eat or drink again until the kingdom of God comes.* The greatest difference between passages is that John doesn't include an account of Jesus instituting the sacrament. Give participants time to think about why these differences exist. Answers could include *different writers, accounts written at different times, the emphasis of the writer, etc.*

Be ready to talk about why John's Gospel is so different than the other passages in this exercise. The Fourth Gospel contains stories such as the changing of water to wine (John 2), the feeding of the five thousand (John 6), and the washing of the disciples' feet (John 13). John assumes that Christians who are already familiar with the

Lord's Supper will understand these miracles to be foreshadowings of the sacrament.

❸ Ask volunteers to share responses. Christ's presence in the Lord's Supper brings us forgiveness and new life. This leads to reconciliation, not only with God, but with others as well.

Conclude with another song or two. Suggestions: *WOV 761, 722.*

Small Group Stuff

Dismiss the groups for Small Group Stuff (the "ride home" portion of the session in small groups) and let them know what time to return for Wrap-up. Relax.

Wrap-up

Remind participants not to violate any confidences in talking about their small group time together with the larger group.

Ask participants what insights they gained into the Lutheran understanding of the Lord's Supper as they talked in their small groups. What questions do they still have?

It is quite possible that some will be confused or troubled by the idea of Christ's presence in the sacrament, either in terms of wanting a simply symbolic interpretation, or conversely, wanting an interpretation focused more on the "stuff"—on changes in the bread and wine into special substances. Acknowledge that Christians of various traditions have struggled with the mystery of how Christ fulfills his promise to be present for us in this meal, but that our task is primarily to obey Christ's command to "do this" and to trust the promise that, in some special way, Christ is present "for you" when we eat and drink.

Be sure to announce the reading for the next session: *The Lutheran Handbook*, page 156 and pages 134–137.

Suggestion for a closing song: *WOV 721.*

THE THREE MOST REBELLIOUS THINGS JESUS DID

Overview *(background and orientation just for you as the leader)*

Just as the Bible is God's Word for you, so too is Jesus. Christianity makes an exclusive claim about Jesus. We believers say that this person who lived in the Roman provinces of Galilee and Judea two thousand years ago is "Lord." We say it flat out: "Jesus is God." If you want to get to know God, then the place to look is in Jesus. He is our down-to-earth God. If one says Jesus isn't God or that he isn't really human, the mystery of his whole being has been missed. For Jesus is the link between God and human beings. The creeds make this clear, and Luther is similarly clear in his explanation to the Second Article of the Creed in his *Small Catechism* (*The Lutheran Handbook*, p. 204), "I believe that Jesus Christ, true God, begotten of the Father in eternity, and also true human being, born of the virgin Mary, is my Lord." Even though Jesus was part of a particular time and place, he is also Lord of all time and all places. Jesus didn't just live two thousand years ago; he's also present as God's work and will in creation from the beginning and into eternity. Open any of the Gospels to a random page, and you'll find a fully connected Jesus. Jesus is absolutely aware of the world around him. He feels the deep human longing for healing, wholeness, and unburdened life in those who come to him. Yet this same Jesus is the transcendent Ruler of the universe. Like all of God's Word, Jesus comes to us as both law and gospel. He has harsh words for the pious (the Pharisees and their modern counterparts) and a message of forgiveness, hope, and new life for those who have tasted

Even though Jesus was part of a particular time and place, he is also Lord of all time and all places. Jesus didn't just live two thousand years ago; he's also present as God's work and will in creation from the beginning and into eternity.

life's bitterness (which is all of us, as we see when the law drives us to be totally honest with ourselves). In Christ, we sinners are liberated from sin, death, and the devil. No longer does our sinful past haunt us. Nor can the grave that lies waiting for each of us ever burden us again, for Jesus provides a future of hope, of mercy, of release.

Preparation

Objective: Each participant will understand the dual nature of Christ as truly human and truly divine as the necessary precondition for his role as redeemer of humanity.

Materials needed: images of Jesus for display (see Table Talk), copies of the Table Talk questions for Session 5 (p. 106), a copy of *The Lutheran Handbook* and workbook for each participant.

Prepare yourself for the session: Read through all the Session 5 material in this leader book and the workbook. Also view the video presentation and commercial in advance.

Prepare the room: Have the video presentation set up, make sure everything works, that it is properly cued, and ready to play. Also have the Video Commercials DVD on hand.

Table Talk

Go to your favorite Internet search engine to locate some images of Jesus suitable to print out (the search term "Jesus" yields over 800,000 to choose from at http://images.google.com). Try to pick out a variety of images, some traditional and some very offbeat or provocative. If the Internet is not available, your church library may have a number of possibilities, or the reference librarian at your public library will be happy to help you. Place six or eight printouts or photocopies of artwork depicting Jesus on each table before participants arrive. In addition, photocopy page 106 and place one card at each table.

Participants will pass the images of Jesus around the table one at a time and discuss the following questions for each:
- What do you recognize as familiar about Jesus in this image?
- What characteristic or trait of Jesus do you see in this image?
- What aspect of Jesus is surprising or unexpected in this image?

Leader Book   45

Large Group Stuff

Opening
Begin with some instrumental music as people are gathering. At the appointed beginning time, have the group sing something lively, then livelier still, then begin to settle into a more mellow mood. Some suggestions for this session are *LBW* 514, 558, 552, 529, 518.

Have a brief reading from scripture. Suggestion for this session: John 12:20-33.

Pray. Participants may be invited to offer petitions. Conclude with your own prayer thanking God for the gift of the gospel of Christ.

Introduction
Briefly introduce the video presenter as Barbara Rossing, Professor of New Testament at the Lutheran School of Theology at Chicago. Before joining the seminary's faculty, Rossing was acting director for Global Mission Interpretation for the American Lutheran Church, pastor at Holden Village Retreat Center, Chelan, Washington, and chaplain at Harvard University Divinity School. She has lectured and preached widely in the Evangelical Lutheran Church in America (ELCA), including keynote lectures at Women of the ELCA theological conferences, global mission events, and synod assemblies. Her articles have appeared in magazines such as *Dialog, Currents in Theology and Mission, Lutheran Standard, The Lutheran,* and *Lutheran Woman Today.*

Point out question 1 in Large Group Stuff in the workbook (p. 24) and prepare participants to follow along.

Jesus was someone who loved to eat, an activity he often undertook with sinners.

Session 5

The title of this session is "The Three Most Rebellious Things Jesus Did" (see *The Lutheran Handbook*, p. 156), but the video and discussion will cover more than this. Make the point that Barbara Rossing will talk about the life of the earthly Jesus and how he rebelled, but she will also speak about the meaning of Jesus for her life, and for each of our lives as believers. These two things are inseparable for Christians—the very human Jesus of history and the divine Jesus we encounter through faith. Both are the same person, truly human and truly God.

Point out the cartoon on p. 25 in the Workbook. Rossing refers to this cartoon in her presentation.

And now a word from our sponsor: In this session's video commercial, Martin "Winkie" Luther is suffering from a terrible illness. "Katie Lu" quickly diagnoses it as a bad case of "affluenza," the distress and lack of fulfillment brought about by affluence and the accumulation of too much material wealth. Fortunately, Katie also knows the cure—the "Balm of Gilead," or the healing power of the Gospel.

Video
Play the video presentation. Then play the commercial for "Balm of Gilead."

Workbook
(Note: the first two workbook pages in each session are for use during the large group time, and the second two pages for each session are for the small group time.)

Ask if there are any initial questions or reactions to the video presentation and commercial (see p. 48).

❶ Ask for volunteers to share what they wrote in the blanks in the workbook. *There are no wrong answers* to these questions, but what the authors had in mind would be something like this:

- As Lutherans, we emphasize Jesus' *gracious presence, down-to-earth stories, humanity.*
- The ministry of Jesus on earth emphasized *healing and renewal, hope, abundance, etc.*
- We're missing something if we focus only on *miracles, atonement, the supernatural, etc.*
- When we welcome Jesus into our hearts *he brings the world, his friends, us into God's heart, etc.*

Leader Book 47

- If Jesus isn't still controversial it's because *we've watered him down, missed something.*

❷ Invite responses from those willing to volunteer their thoughts. Rossing's point is that there is more to Jesus' life than these bare facts. Note that if others did not agree, the Gospels Matthew, Mark, Luke, and John would never have been written! But these essentials have been central for Christians through the ages because they emphasize both the human and divine natures of Jesus.

❸ Luther's explanation of the Second Article of the creed first points out the humanity and divinity of Jesus. Then Luther describes the work of Jesus as *redeeming us and purchasing and freeing us from sin, death, and the devil.*

❹ The "Balm of Gilead," the healing power of the Gospel, reminds Luther to depend on Christ, not on the accumulation of material wealth. You might ask participants if they believe "affluenza" is a serious problem today.

Conclude with another song or two. Suggestions: *LBW* 530, 458.

Small Group Stuff

Dismiss the groups for Small Group Stuff (the "ride home" portion of the session in small groups) and let them know what time to return for Wrap-up. Relax.

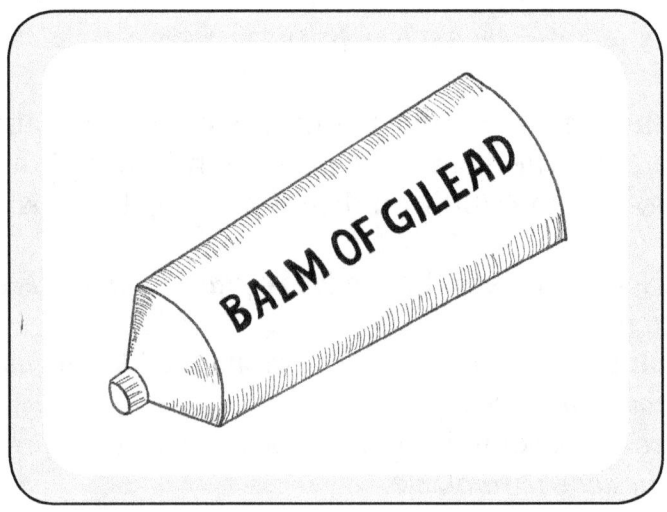

As seen in the video commercial, the Balm of Gilead relieves symptoms of affluenza so you can enjoy faith in Jesus Christ.

Session 5

Wrap-up

Remind participants not to violate any confidences in talking about their small group time together with the larger group.

Ask participants what insights they gained into the person of Jesus as they talked in their small groups. What questions do they still have?

Be sensitive to the fact that some may have difficulty focusing on the human side of Jesus, while there may be others who struggle with the notion of Jesus as divine. Hear any concerns that are raised, but simply restate that a savior who can do what the New Testament claims must be both human and divine.

Be sure to announce the reading for the next session: *The Lutheran Handbook*, pages 145–146, 168–169, and 175–176.

Suggestion for a closing song: *LBW* 363.

Copyright © Daniel W. Erlander. Used by permission.

Leader Book 49

HOW TO READ THE BIBLE

Overview (*background and orientation just for you as the leader*)

Lutherans see God speaking to human sinners in three ways: in the scriptures, in the crucified and risen Lord Jesus Christ, and in proclamation. In The Lutheran Course, we take up each aspect of God's Word in turn. To the uneducated, the Bible is merely smudges of ink on a stack of pages. But, first of all, our brains have been trained to regard those smudges of ink as words and thoughts and ideas. Secondly, the Holy Spirit uses those thoughts and ideas to speak to sinners so that the words become a living Word. In the video presentation, Rolf Jacobson gives us the analogy that the Bible is like a newspaper, containing many different types of stories and different types of articles. What links the sixty-six books of the Bible together is that they came out of the real lives of God's people. The Bible is a community library. Just as we read each part of the newspaper differently—or different books from the community library differently—when we read the Bible we must mentally adjust our interpretation according to the type of literature we are reading at the moment.

In our day, people often ask whether we ought to read the Bible literally or figuratively. But these categories aren't very helpful or very Lutheran. The Holy Spirit uses each type of literature in the Bible to speak faithfully in its own way. When God's Word in the Bible functions as law and gospel, that's when it's doing its proper job. The authority of the Bible does not come from its literal rendering

The Holy Spirit uses each type of literature in the Bible to speak faithfully in its own way.

of the thoughts of people long dead, but from its power to call us to life here and now. There are challenges to reading the Bible in ways that call us to faith. Some challenges are real, such as the differences in language and culture between Bible writers and our own society. Other challenges are artificial, such as the notion that the Bible is so complicated that only experts can understand it, or that the Bible is full of contradictions. The Bible is the church's book, and we use it best when we read it in worship and community, so we are able to discern law and gospel together.

Preparation

Objective: Each participant will understand that the Bible is a collection of writings from many people over many centuries that speak to Christians in various ways to call us to faith. Further, each participant will understand that, while challenging, understanding the Bible is not something exclusive to experts, but is the task of the church in community.

Materials needed: anything necessary for singing (instruments, songbooks, etc.), copies of the Table Talk questions for Session 6 (pp. 107–108), and a copy of *The Lutheran Handbook* and workbook for each participant.

Prepare yourself for the session: Read through all the Session 6 material in this leader book and the workbook. Also view the video presentation and commercial in advance.

Prepare the room: Have the video presentation set up, make sure everything works, that it is properly cued, and ready to play. Also have the Video Commercials DVD on hand.

Table Talk

Photocopy the Table Talk questions on pages 107–108. Place a set of cards face down on each table where participants will sit as they gather or eat. For each Bible passage, participants should share answers to the discussion questions: What does this passage say to me about the Bible? How does this passage challenge me about how I use the Bible?

Repeat the process until time is up.

Large Group Stuff

Opening
Begin with some instrumental music as people are gathering. At the appointed beginning time, have the group sing something lively, then livelier still, then begin to settle into a more mellow mood. Some suggestions for this session are *WOV* 716, 684, 712, 650, 776.

Have a brief reading from scripture. Suggestion for this session: Romans 10:8-17.

Pray. Participants may be invited to offer petitions. Conclude with your own prayer thanking God for the gift of the gospel of Christ.

Introduction
Briefly introduce the video presenter as Rolf A. Jacobson, Assistant Professor of Old Testament at Luther Seminary in St. Paul, Minnesota. He is the author of the book, *'Many Are Saying': The Function of Direct Discourse in the Hebrew Psalter*, writer for the No Experience Necessary Bible study series, and serves as the Associate Editor of *Word & World*, a journal for pastors and Bible scholars.

Point out question 1 in Large Group Stuff in the workbook (p. 28) and prepare participants to follow along. Explain that Jacobson begins by briefly reemphasizing what *The Lutheran Handbook* says about the Bible: It is not a single book but a collection of different writings by a variety of authors spanning over a thousand years of experiences. Jacobson will point out several challenges or "hurdles" that often make the Bible intimidating for readers. Ask participants to note these challenges, and also to think about which of these are hurdles for them personally.

And now a word from our sponsor: In this session's video commercial, ""Katie Lu" strains to read the Bible until Martin "Winkie" Luther gives her a brand new "Hermeneutic-COOL" Bible reading glass. (*Hermeneutics* is the word theologians use for the process of interpreting religious writings.) It was in long and careful study of the Bible that the real Martin Luther came to understand the need for the Reformation some 500 years ago.

Video
Play the video presentation. Then play the commercial for the "Hermeneuti-COOL magnifying glass."

Workbook

Note: The first two workbook pages in each session are for Large Group Stuff (large group use), and the next two pages in each session are for Small Group Stuff (small group use).

Ask if there are any initial questions or reactions to the video presentation and commercial (see p. 54).

❶ Ask for volunteers to share what they wrote in the blanks in the workbook. *There are no wrong answers* to the first three questions, but what the authors had in mind would be something like this:

- In terms of the variety of literature it contains, the Bible can be compared to *a newspaper, a library, etc.*
- What's different about the way Lutherans read the Bible is *We read it through the "lens" of justification by faith, We look for law and gospel, etc.*
- For Lutherans, the Bible's authority comes from *what the words do here and now, etc.*

The following have answers that were provided by the video presentation.

Four hurdles in reading the Bible are:
- *Cultural distance*
- *The assumption that the Bible is for experts*
- *Contradictions within the Bible*
- *Language differences*

Three ways to use the Bible effectively are:
- *In worship*
- *In groups*
- *Just start*

❷ You will probably not have time to work through all of these passages, but select a few. Note that there are a few that most Lutherans would not read literally (Matthew 5:29, for example), but there is some gospel to be found in each and every example!

Let participants know it's not necessary to choose between reading the Bible literally or figuratively. God's truth is revealed both through literal and figurative language.

Leader Book 53

❸ Encourage participants to be creative with their responses (for example, a tool to help us understand the Bible or perhaps one that would make sure we took time to read the Bible on our own regularly). Many people have difficulty reading the Bible because they are constantly looking for hidden spiritual meanings, but Luther taught that straightforward interpretation is best.

Conclude with another song or two. Suggestions: *WOV 779, 770.*

Small Group Stuff

Dismiss the groups for Small Group Stuff (the "ride home" portion of the session in small groups) and let them know what time to return for Wrap-up. Relax.

As seen in the video commercial, the Hermeneuti-COOL brand magnifying glass helps you discover the source of a literary work, study its composition, determine its date, and trace its influence throughout the ages.

Session 6

Wrap-up

Remind participants not to violate any confidences in talking about their small group time together with the larger group.

Ask participants what insights they gained into the Bible as they talked in their small groups. What questions do they still have?

It is quite possible that some will insist that a literal interpretation of scripture is the only acceptable way of reading the Bible. Explain that in the Lutheran tradition there has always been room for a wide diversity of interpretations, but where Lutherans always stand together is in reading the Bible through the lens of the gospel of God's grace.

Be sure to announce the reading for the next session: *The Lutheran Handbook*, pages 89–90 and 105–106.

Suggestion for a closing song: *WOV 725*.

HOW TO SHARE YOUR FAITH WITH SOMEONE

Overview *(background and orientation just for you as the leader)*

An evangelist is a sinner who's been hit by God's mission in Christ and can't resist telling others about it. Evangelism isn't just one item on a smorgasbord of religious activities for the properly pious to put on their plates. Evangelism is central because we've been grasped by Jesus, who is so in love with the world that he won't leave us or it unchanged. The freedom that sinners gain in an encounter with Jesus always brings about a new obedience to God. Thus, evangelism isn't optional, and it isn't a sideline, but is *the* mission of the church. Christ's aim isn't to build an institution called "the church," but to use this gathering of forgiven sinners to bring good news to the world. As Kelly Fryer asserts in the video, "The church exists entirely for the sake of people who aren't in it yet." The goal is not institutional survival, but the sharing of good news. And the best place that happens is in everyday life with the people you encounter on a regular basis. This means that setting up a distinction between those inside the church and those outside the church isn't very helpful. This unhelpful distinction assumes that once you've got faith you've got it for good and all you need is a job description for how to go out and bring in more outsiders. But, as Lutherans, we know that we remain both saint and sinner until the grave. Even the most regular church goers or faithful Bible readers are still sinners who continually need the gospel flowing from Jesus' vine into their branches. The church, after all, is simply a gathering of sinners who have been grasped by

Evangelism isn't optional, and it isn't a sideline, but is the *mission of the church.*

the same reality: there's no life to be had without Jesus. Thus, the church's entire mission is to be a bearer of the gospel for the sake of those who have not yet heard it, as well as those who desperately need to hear it again.

Preparation

Objective: Each participant will understand the close connection between receiving the gift of grace offered through faith in Christ, and the command to "go and make disciples" by sharing the gospel with others.

Materials needed: anything necessary for singing (instruments, songbooks, etc.), "table tents" for Table Talk (p. 109) and a copy of *The Lutheran Handbook* and workbook for each participant. Have copies of the course evaluation form (p. 110) ready to distribute at Wrap-up.

Prepare yourself for the session: Read the Session 7 material in the leader book and workbook, and view the video presentation and commercial in advance.

Prepare the room: Have the video presentation set up, make sure everything works, that it is properly cued, and ready to play. Also have the Video Commercials DVD on hand.

Table Talk

Place a "table tent" on each table before participants gather. By now, Table Talk should come naturally and it shouldn't take more than these few items to get participants talking until the time is up.

Large Group Stuff

Opening
Begin with some instrumental music as people are gathering. At the appointed beginning time, have the group sing something lively, then livelier still, then begin to settle into a more mellow mood. Some suggestions for this session are *WOV* 752, 754, 770, 764, 756.

Have a brief reading from scripture. Suggestion for this session: Matthew 28:16-20.

Pray. Participants may be invited to offer petitions. Conclude with your own prayer thanking God for the gift of the gospel of Christ.

Introduction
Briefly introduce the video presenter as Kelly A. Fryer, Executive Director of ARE: A Renewal Enterprise. Fryer is in demand as a consultant to congregational and synodical leaders, and has a full speaking schedule at synodical and churchwide events across the country. She was a member of the ELCA's "task force on evangelism" and has served as a member of the Transformational Ministries Team of the ELCA (Division for Outreach). She is the author of *Reclaiming the "C" Word: Daring to Be Church Again* (Augsburg Fortress, 2006), *Reclaiming the "L" Word: Renewing the Church from Its Lutheran Core* (Augsburg Fortress, 2003), the No Experience Necessary Bible study series (Augsburg Fortress, 2005), and several other books and articles.

Point out question 1 in Large Group Stuff in the workbook (p. 32) and prepare participants to follow along.

Explain that Kelly Fryer will echo many key points that participants have heard before in The Lutheran Course: She will speak about law and gospel, and will underscore the Lutheran emphasis on the gift of grace. However, she will take the additional step of challenging participants with the "so what?" question. Fryer points to evangelism as the natural and urgent consequence of experiencing the grace of God in Christ.

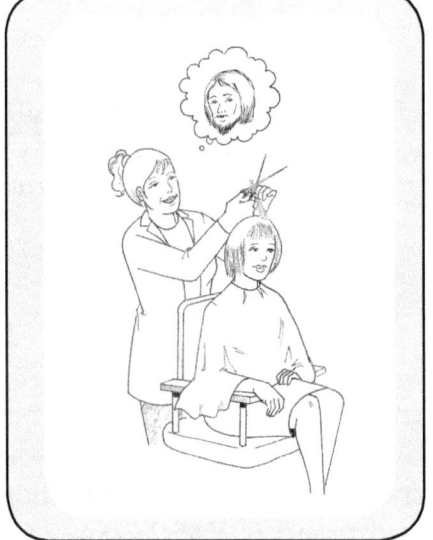

Being an evangelizing Christian should not be confused with being extroverted or loud. Shy, retiring Lutherans are often among the church's most effective evangelizing individuals.

Session 7

And now a word from our sponsor: In this session's video commercial, Martin "Winkie" Luther is suffering from a bad case of laryngitis from so much preaching. "Katie Lu" offers a solution in the "Go Tell It on the Mountain brand Gospel-spreading megaphone."

Video
Play the video presentation. Then play the commercial for the "Go Tell It on the Mountain" megaphone.

Workbook
Note: The first two workbook pages in each session are for Large Group Stuff (large group use), and the next two pages in each session are for Small Group Stuff (small group use).

Ask if there are any initial questions or reactions to the video presentation and commercial (see below). Did the presenter's passion for the mission of the church push any participants beyond their comfort level?

❶ Ask for volunteers to share what they wrote in the blanks in the workbook. *There are no wrong answers* to these questions, but what the authors had in mind would be something like this:

- Lutherans understand evangelism *to be inseparable from God's mission, our main task, etc.*
- When you meet Jesus, *you want to tell others, it changes your life, etc.*
- We can't separate *the gift from the call, salvation from service to our neighbor, etc.*
- The church exists *for mission, for the sake of the people who aren't in it yet, etc.*
- The real truth about evangelists is that they *love people, dare to speak up, etc.*

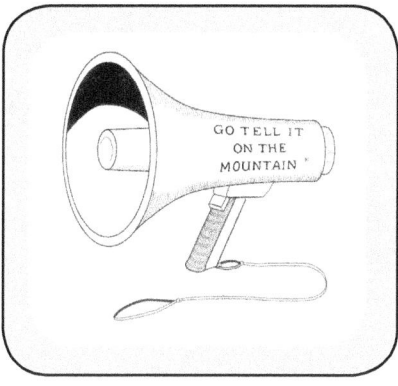

As seen in the video commercial, Go Tell It on the Mountain brand Gospel-spreading megaphones get God's Word out to all the world.

Leader Book 59

❷ Peter, Paul, and Mary: Give participants a few minutes to do this matching exercise individually, then ask for volunteers to share their answers. Read John 21:1-17, Acts 9:1-18, and John 20:11-18 out loud to the group, or encourage participants to read these passages at home.

Figure	Encounter with the Risen Lord	Result
Simon Peter (John 21:1-17, Acts 2:14-40)	A. On the road to Damascus	1. Was the first to tell the good news that Christ is risen
Saul/Paul (Acts 9:1-18)	B. Just outside the empty tomb	2. The first Christian preacher on the day of Pentecost
Mary Magdalene (John 20:11-18)	C. At a breakfast on the beach	3. Was turned from a chief persecutor of Christians into one of Christ's main ambassadors

Answers: Simon Peter: C, 2; Saul/Paul: A, 3; Mary Magdalene: B, 1.

Note: The risen Lord speaks directly to Simon Peter on the beach (John 21:1-17), but there are other accounts in which Peter, as one of the disciples, encounters him. In John's Gospel, Christ appears to the disciples in a locked house (20:19-23) and appears again a week later and speaks with Thomas (20:24-29). In Matthew, the risen Lord meets the eleven disciples in Galilee (28:16-20). In the longer ending of Mark, Christ appears to the eleven (16:14-18). In Luke, Peter runs to the tomb and finds it empty (24:12), the disciples say the Lord has appeared to Peter (24:34), and Jesus appears to all of the disciples (24:36-49).

❸ "Winkie" needed a megaphone to continue to share the faith. What do we need? Get participants to start thinking about this and about what prevents them from sharing their faith. More discussion will follow in the small groups.

Conclude with another song or two. Suggestions: *WOV* 650, 765.

Small Group Stuff

Dismiss the groups for Small Group Stuff (the "ride home" portion of the session in small groups) and let them know what time to return for Wrap-up. Relax.

Wrap-up

Remind participants not to violate any confidences in talking about their small group time together with the larger group.

Ask participants what insights they gained into the Lutheran understanding of evangelism as they talked in their small groups. What questions do they still have?

It is quite possible that there will be mild or even considerable resistance to the notion of evangelizing. Ask the group what further steps they would like to take to become more comfortable with this aspect of Christian life and calling. What next steps are the small groups contemplating?

Thank all those who have contributed to this course, including the publicist, musician(s), Table Talk coordinator, small group leaders, and the participants.

Distribute the course evaluation form, and give participants a few quiet moments to complete it before they leave.

Suggestion for a closing song: *WOV* 651.

PRESENTERS

James A. Nestingen (Session 1) is Professor Emeritus of Church History at Luther Seminary, St. Paul, Minnesota, and author of numerous books, including *Martin Luther: His Life and Teachings* (Wipf & Stock, 2004), *Martin Luther: A Life* (Augsburg Books, 2003), and *Manger in the Mountains* (Augsburg Fortress, 1999).

Kenneth Sundet Jones (Session 2) is Assistant Professor of Philosophy and Religion at Grand View College, Des Moines, Iowa, and contributor to *Word and World*, *The Lutheran Quarterly*, *The Lutheran Handbook* (Augsburg Fortress, 2005), and Here We Stand confirmation curriculum (Augsburg Fortress).

Winston D. Persaud (Session 3) is Professor of Systematic Theology at Wartburg Seminary, Dubuque, Iowa. His publications include *The Theology of the Cross and Marx's Anthropology: A View from the Caribbean* (Peter Lang, 1991) and numerous articles and essays.

Foster R. McCurley (Session 4) is former Dean of the Faculty and Professor of Old Testament and Hebrew at Lutheran Theological Seminary, Philadelphia, Pennsylvania. His books include *Wrestling with the Word: Christian Preaching from the Hebrew Bible* (Morehouse, 1996).

Barbara R. Rossing (Session 5) is Professor of New Testament at the Lutheran School of Theology, Chicago, Illinois, and author of *The Rapture Exposed: The Message of Hope in the Book of Revelation* (Westview Press, 2005) and *The Choice Between Two Cities: Whore, Bride, and Empire in the Apocalypse* (Trinity Press International, 1999).

Rolf A. Jacobson (Session 6) is Assistant Professor of Old Testament at Luther Seminary, St. Paul, Minnesota, and writer of the No Experience Necessary Bible study series with Kelly A. Fryer.

Kelly A. Fryer (Session 7) is Executive Director of ARE: A Renewal Enterprise, lead writer of the No Experience Necessary Bible study series, contributing editor of *A Story Worth Sharing: Engaging Evangelism* (Augsburg Fortress, 2004), and author of *Reclaiming the "C" Word: Daring to Be Church Again* (Augsburg Fortress, 2006), and *Reclaiming the "L" Word: Renewing the Church from Its Lutheran Core* (Augsburg Fortress, 2003).

HOW TO TELL THE DIFFERENCE BETWEEN THE LAW AND THE GOSPEL

James A. Nestingen

The Lutheran Proposal

First of all, the Lutheran proposal is to interpret all of scripture in light of the promise made in Christ Jesus. When Lutherans say "justification by faith," the term has two references:

❶ *Being aligned*
One is being true or being aligned or being placed in a proper relationship. When Luther talked about it, he used a beautiful phrase. He used to speak of being made what Adam and Eve were meant to be, only better. That is, he spoke of being realigned out of the distortions of life and being placed in a proper relationship with God with the neighbor so that alignment is proper once more.

❷ *Declaring Christ Jesus as the subject of the verb*
At the second level of the doctrine of justification is a set of rules for setting out the promise of the gospel so that it speaks of declaring Christ Jesus as the subject of the verb so that Christ is always the worker. It speaks as identifying the hearer as the direct object so that the hearer is the beneficiary of Christ's work. It speaks with declaring this unconditionally so that the gift is being bestowed, not as a possibility but as a reality. It speaks of this happening right now in the present tense. For instance, when Jesus goes to Lazarus's tomb, Mary says to him, "Yes, Lord, I know that he will rise again on the last day." Jesus answers, "No, I am the resurrection and the life right here." [See John 11:17-25.]

Spot the Difference

So one way to distinguish is to look at the language. You can spot the difference at a preliminary level by looking at the language. The law generally comes in the imperative voice. It says, "Do this" and "Don't do that. Stop it. Cut it out. If I catch you again . . ." It is stern and it has a pointed finger. If-then, if-then, if-then.

The gospel, on the other hand, comes in promises. Unconditional faith. Here is one that is my favorite: No one will snatch you out of my hand [see John 10:28]. No one will snatch you out of my hand. There is not a condition there. There is no condition—explicit or implicit. There is a promise. Here is another one: Nothing will separate you from the love of God in Christ Jesus our Lord. There it is, bare-naked. Nothing. Nothing.

I remember the first time that I went to call on a dying person when I was an intern. It was in Spokane, Washington. The lady's name was Emma Hoopie. She was in her 80s. My mother had given me a wonderful sport jacket that was made by a tailor in Saskatchewan. It was made for Saskatchewan weather. It was 92 degrees when I went to the hospital and I was standing in the hospital with sweat seeping down my back, trying to talk to this lady scared to death of death, and scared to death of her and scared to death of everything and uncertain of my vocation and wondering. I took out my little pocket testament and said, "Miss Hoopie, I am going to read something to you." I started into that passage from Romans 8: Nothing will separate you from the love of God in Christ Jesus Lord. Nothing. Not height or death, principalities or powers, things present or things to come. Nothing in all creation. [See Romans 8:38-39.] There on the lips of a trembling intern, there in the ears of a dying woman, the gospel exploded. It's excessive. It's power. It bestows the gift of life in the presence of death. Bestows a new future. So you listen to the grammar.

Opinio Legis?

Deep in the human heart there is a superstition that, in the language of Lutheranism, is called the *opinio legis*. The *opinio legis* is the secret conviction of the heart that finally the law has the last word, that somewhere there is a recipe for life, and that if you get it right, you will be right—and that if you get it right, you will live happily ever after. Your teeth won't rot. You will never experience erectile dysfunction or any similar failing of the human frame. Everything will work, right? So the *opinio legis* is the premise that we generally work from. Like Bill Cosby says, "There is no such thing as an atheist." When the elevator starts to drop, everybody folds their hands. So when George Gallup does his polls, he finds people all over the country that have no connection whatsoever with any kind of a church but who pray—regularly, in emergencies, but also habitually, apparently. That is the *opinio legis*. That somehow there is a power out there—that if I get it right with that power, I'll be okay.

The gospel of Christ Jesus exposes that word. It exposes that as a superstition. The gospel says that Moses is dead and Christ has risen. The gospel says that the *opinio legis* is a fraud. The gospel says that you're never going to get it right. If you do get it right you'll finally be wrong, right? You see? So it is the gospel that requires the law-gospel distinction. If you don't make the distinction, the law will take over everything.

If-Then, Because-Therefore . . .

In a wonderful book called *Lutheranism: The Theological Movement and Its Confessional Writings*, Eric Gritsch and Robert Jenson define them in this way: Law is constructed on the basis of "if-then" statements. *If* you eat all your vegetables, you will get your dessert. The *if* names a condition that is to be fulfilled. The *then* names the result of the fulfillment of the condition. So if you drive 55 miles an hour you will arrive at your destination without a ticket. If you drive 65 miles an hour, under the theory that I was told, they would give you 10 miles for free. You may or may not arrive without a ticket. That is, law is practically if-then. The gospel language, as Jenson proposes this definition, is "because-therefore" language. Because Christ loves you, your sin is forgiven. In the if-then of the law, you're cast back on yourself to fulfill the condition. In because-therefore language, Christ has fulfilled the condition and, therefore, the benefit is yours. So that if-then language drives you back to yourself. Because-therefore, the language of the gospel, frees you to enter into the relationships of life. You are now held in Christ. Christ is fulfilling and because he's fulfilled that condition involved in the *because, therefore* you're free.

What Does the Law Do?

So the question then becomes, "What does law do?" And the Lutheran answer to that question is that law, while it cannot save, can do a couple of things:

❶ *Keeps order and restrains*
One, it can keep order. So if you are coming over a hill and see a car sitting off to the side far ahead of you, instinctively you pull your

foot off the foot feed, of course. There is a distinct possibility that is a policeman sitting there waiting for you. The law will restrain. It will force you to ask a question, "What am I doing?" Maybe you are driving along 75 to 80 miles an hour, listening to the radio, and paying no attention to anything, and all of a sudden that car is there for no apparent reason. The law restrains.

❷ Attacks the conscience

At the second level, the law has an incredible capacity to get loose in the conscience. That is to get loose in the sense of yourself. Once it gets loose in your sense of yourself, then it attacks. It says, "You did this and you enjoyed it. You did this and you would do it again if you had the chance, and you are thinking about further opportunities. You did this and it's in your nature to do this. You have always done this." Do you see how it's accelerating? The law will go from the specific event, the specific situation, the specific circumstance to your person and once it has gotten hold of your person ("I have always done things like this"), it expands into the past and present and lays claims to everything you see. So the art of distinguishing law and gospel is the art of recognizing what's ultimate and what's penultimate.

The law is always premised on death and shortage. The law is always premised on conditions that have to be fulfilled. The law says, "What if? Do this. If you don't, you must, just think what will happen if you do not. You're going to get it. You're going to run out. There's going to be trouble. Do this, do this, do this." Law after law after law compounding itself, if-then, if-then, if-then.

The gospel is spontaneous, excessive, explosive. So I will give you life and I will give it abundantly. Do you see the gospel? Because the gospel is premised on the work of Christ, rather than on the presence of shortage or condition, it starts to spill over into everything.

Christ Will Not Fail Me

Early yesterday morning I had breakfast with two of my closest friends. They are both in their late 70s. Because I am going on sabbatical we had breakfast together so that we could say goodbye. I will not see them for a while, for a year. I love them both dearly. They have both been through big-time illness. One has had to put his wife in the nursing home because of Alzheimer's and she is not eating and so her death is approaching. The other lost his 45-year-old daughter

Transcript 1

a month ago. So the three of us sat eating breakfast and one of them said this. He said, "You know, if I had to depend on my own faith at this point, I'd be in total despair, but Christ is at work in me—through his work encouraging, strengthening, comforting, giving me life. So that as I face the loss of my wife I know that a new future will emerge out of his hands." The other one said, "He is the resurrection and the life. He is, and so my daughter rests with him now. We had her for 45 years. We wanted more! We wanted more but Christ has her now, and so we rest in that."

That kind of faith is not achieved. That kind of faith is not something you set up on management by objective. It's not something you get for crying in the night. You know, it happens. In the Word it happens, and when it happens it grips even as you are being torn apart by the shape of life, even as you are going down with Christ, being crucified with him. So that when you look at yourself all you see is loss and when you look at yourself all you see is what's being torn away. It's being torn away—he's giving himself in his typically excessive way, pouring himself out, laying himself down with you, for you. So that then faith emerges, not as an impossible condition, but it emerges rather as the resurrection of the dead in this life—hope.

So my friend said, "Christ is present now under the sign of hope. He will not fail me."

FIVE THINGS YOU SHOULD KNOW ABOUT THE LUTHERAN REFORMATION

Ken Sundet Jones

Luther arose in the middle of what historians call the late medieval era. It's a turning point in history. Luther was born in 1483. The Renaissance had already begun in the south in Italy, and was moving up the European continent. But that whole era—the shift from what historians call the late medieval era to the early modern era, was happening right when Luther was alive. And his participation in the events during that era helped shape and change everything that happened in Europe, in America, in the whole west, in terms of our thinking—especially in terms of the church. The church that we have today would not be in existence if it hadn't been for Luther.

The late medieval times—you know, they call them the Dark Ages, and rightfully so. You can see it in *The Lutheran Handbook* (Augsburg Fortress, 2005). There's a great little section in there about what life in the medieval times was like. It was nasty, brutish, and short. There were times in those centuries when the life expectancy for a person would be about 16 years. So we'd be dead if it were us.

Luther's Life

Well, if we're going to talk about Luther's private life—his personal life—you have to start back at his roots. He wasn't a member of the nobility. He wasn't part of the power elite in any way. He was the son of a coal mining family of some kind. And he came out of that and got an education. He was going to be a lawyer, and something happened to him while he was studying at the University of Erfurt. We don't know what happened. The best scholars can figure out is that he was having some doubts about what he wanted to do with his life. And apparently he'd been home to his parents' house and was heading back to the University and got caught in a thunderstorm, and lightning struck nearby. He wrote about this later in his life. And he cried out to Saint Anne, who was the mother of the Virgin Mary, to help them. And he said, "I will become a monk."

And so he became a monk in the Augustinian hermitage, much to his father's consternation. And he was an avid monk. He was scrupulous about it. He never went halfway on anything. He went whole hog. He went to penance. He went to confess to his Orders Superior, Johann von Staupitz, and he wanted to make sure every last sin was confessed so that he could be shriven—he could be clean of all that sin that kept hanging on him after his baptism.

And he'd constantly go to Staupitz to confess those sins to try to slough off those doubts and temptations. And finally one day, Staupitz said to him, "Luther, you come to me confessing and confessing and confessing all the time, and it's such little stuff. Every time you fart," he said, "you come to me to confess your sin for doing that. I want you to go away from me and actually commit some real sin before you come back, because you know Christ is your Lord, and you haven't trusted him to take care of you, to take care of your sin. And because of that you're falling prey to all these other temptations."

I think that that was a significant thing for Luther that Staupitz started. Staupitz planted a seed in Luther's head somehow. And then when you combine that with Luther's later work as a professor teaching Bible, everything finally came together.

And Luther's order also saw to it that he got an education. He got his master's degree and his doctorate. And they decided that he should go teach. So they sent him to this little town of Wittenberg.

Luther Discovers the Gospel

Luther was a Bible scholar who did his job like any theologian worth her or his salt should be—at least a Christian theologian—because as Christians we are tied to a word. And Luther took his task as a teacher of scripture and a preacher of God's word seriously. And I think that enabled him to be ripe for the picking by God.

So the earlier question was, was it just chance that it all happened? I think if we're going to be faithful, we have to say it's not chance. But also that God uses the chances and happenstances of events in history as they come together in our daily lives, that the randomness of it is one of God's great tools. And God used that—all the elements to insert faith into this man in sixteenth-century Germany in a way that broke things open for us pew-sitters today as we're sitting there hoping to hear a word from God. Luther shaped Lutheran preaching in a way that we might hear something good from God, just as he had heard it.

Luther—later in his life as he was looking back on all the events that he'd been through—he talked about having to teach Romans. And that he got to that section in Romans that talks about the righteousness of God and how it horrifying it was for him to think about God's righteousness, because God was righteous and Luther was not. And he knew it very well from his own experience, because he kept trying and trying and trying, over and over and over again, to become righteous, to be better. And he never got better. As much as he tried to be a saint, he kept realizing how deeply he was sinful.

And then it dawned on him. I think it was more gradual than sudden. But he had this realization that the righteousness of God is not something that God bears down on us with, that God burdens us with, but instead it's something that's a righteousness *from* God. It's given to sinners in Christ Jesus. It's imputed, is the proper theological language. It's placed in sinners when there's faith. And when Luther looked back on those events, he said, "I had this realization. And then I went back to scripture and I started reading scripture on those terms. I looked at this passage and this passage and this passage and this passage, and suddenly everything that may have been confusing or muddy or foggy for me somehow changed from nebulous to absolute clarity. This scripture had a point that it was aimed at and directed at. Instead of a word that burdened sinners or wagged a finger at sinners saying, "Shape up, be what I intended you to be"—instead was a word in Christ for the ungodly, for the godless, for the sinner, for you.

Indulgences

So Luther prepared a set of statements about indulgences. Questioning them. Wondering about this, and trying to make an argument on the basis of this newfound theology, this stance that he'd come upon. And there were five less than a hundred. We call them the 95 Theses. The story is that he posted those theses on the door of the castle church in Wittenberg, Germany. If you go there today, it's not a wooden door, it's a bronze door, and the 95 Theses are cast in bronze on that door.

But a miraculous thing happened. Luther's words—apparently he'd also sent them to his bishop—the 95 Theses got out. And what's important to know about that is that this was the decades, you know, sixty years or so, seventy years or so, after Gutenberg's invention of the movable type printing press. And so there were printing presses all over Europe. And there weren't copyright laws like there are today. And so somebody could get a hold of something that Luther had written, take it from Wittenberg, over to Leipzig, over to Jena, down to Augsburg, Nuremberg, Braunschweig, to all those cities. And each place had a printing press, and they could reprint it with impunity and no financial benefit to Luther whatsoever.

And so those 95 theses were broadcast all across Europe. Those kinds of publications became known as *flugschriften* in German, which means "flying letters," because they practically flew across the continent. And people got a hold of this.

So for us today, five hundred years almost from Luther's time, it's important because it matters for sinners. Luther will never matter for somebody who doesn't regard herself or himself as a sinner.

Luther's Death

We should probably talk about Luther's death. He died in 1546, in February. If you look in the front of your *Lutheran Book of Worship* in your list of festivals and you go to February, you will see the date that we commemorate Luther in the church, and we celebrate his life and his faith, and it's not his birthday. It's his death date, like we do with all the saints.

That's the kind of death that Luther died. His friends asked him if he was confident in his salvation, and he said, "Yes, absolutely." And he died in the night. And when they went through his things later—his pockets of his robes—they found a slip of paper on which he had scribbled a few words. And in German they were, "*Wir sind Bettler*": "We are beggars. This is true."

That's kind of a bookend for Luther. The Reformation began with him saying in the 95 Theses: When God asks for repentance, God demands all of life being repentance. Luther ends his life saying we're beggars. We're repenting all the time—again, again, and again. All we have, all we can hope to be, is only bound up in Christ.

THE ANATOMY OF A BAPTISM

Winston D. Persaud

It is appropriate that Lutherans emphasize baptism, because for us baptism is the sacrament of initiation into life in Jesus Christ. And we say it's a sacrament because we take it as being commanded by Jesus (thinking of Matthew 28). It has a promise: forgiveness of sins. And it has a created element: water. And those three facets constitute sacrament: command by Jesus, an element (water), and a promise.

And we see baptism as the experience of this new life, which God alone offers in Jesus Christ. So it is in fact the sacrament which bears or conveys the gracious self-giving of God in Jesus Christ.

Fundamentally, we confess that everyone has turned away from God. We have turned to created things to find life and wholeness, instead of trusting in God, for which we were created. And so we are separated from God. And we ourselves—no human being is capable of healing this brokenness, this broken relationship. And so God is the one who alone can do something about healing this brokenness. And God does that, and has done that, in and through the life, death, and resurrection of Jesus Christ. So what's the benefit? It is new life in God through Jesus Christ. It is the experience of wholeness and forgiveness—reconciliation—the sort of umbrella term that scripture uses. The Christian tradition has used *salvation*, to be saved.

For Lutherans, baptism in a real way is a summary of the gospel. God graciously gives, rather than God gives as a reward. And so when we emphasize baptism, we're emphasizing the gracious self-giving of God in Jesus Christ through the power of the Holy Spirit who calls, gathers, enlightens, and sanctifies. And we are emphasizing that the Spirit who gives this new life of faith, energizes us to live our lives of faith in the world. And so in talking about our relationship with God, we talk about baptism because it is the beginning of that new life that is sustained through the hearing of the Word, and the eating of the bread, and the drinking of the wine.

Water and the Word

Whenever we think of baptism, it is critical for us to remember the tangible character of the water, created means, vehicles through which God comes—always created means, the stuff of life, we might say, and the Word, the Word of promise, the Word who is Jesus Christ who comes in and through and with that water. It is absolutely essential to keep the two together—water and Word, Word and water. And so when we talk about mystical, it is a mystery in the sense that in the paradox of the ordinariness, Jesus Christ—the Word become flesh, is real and present, giving and offering and creating new life. And we need that Word to be said and to be enacted daily.

God's Act for Us

There is something about the sacraments of baptism and holy communion that reminds us that no matter what our condition is before God, whether we have lived pleasing to God, or we have disobeyed and followed our own ways, there's something about those sacraments that remind us fundamentally all of us stand on common ground. There's a leveling.

So, for example, at a baptism to see an adult cry, overcome by the emotion of it all. But overcome also by the experience of the grace of God, and being touched by it. That's a tangible reminder that whether young or old, baby or great-grandparent, we are all on common ground.

To use the image that comes to mind, which Luther used towards the end of his life, we are beggars. That is true. That is true. And it is very touching, as a pastor, to see people well up with tears. One could say, it is the Spirit giving us a gift saying, "Know assuredly we all fundamentally are beggars receiving God's grace."

A Cloud of Witnesses

We need to keep in mind that baptism is a communal event. It's an act of the church. It's an act of the communion of saints. And any attempt at privatizing and making baptism an act which happens within the context of an exclusive group—that violates the very nature of baptism.

We should think of baptism—as with the Lord's Supper, the Holy Communion—as a public act in which the Christian message is being enacted before the world because the new identity we have in Christ is a new identity which is to be lived out publicly in the world. And so when we, in fact, practice baptism, we do so with others present—both those who believe in Jesus and people for whom the Christian message is not the reality in which they live. So those who know the message are reminded of it, and those for whom the message is not the truth about life hear the message, see it enacted. And we are surrounded in the baptism by a cloud of witnesses. We must always attend to the fact that we who ask for baptism of our child, or of ourselves, we don't make baptism what it is. It's God's gift, and when God gives God's gift in Jesus Christ, it's a public gift. It's personal, not impersonal. But I'm drawing the distinction between the public nature of the gift over against circumscribing it and making it private and privatized, and even sort of an exclusive commodity, which violates the gift.

Our Response

There is, of course, the expectation that one lives one's life consistent with the promise—not everything goes. At the same time one can't legislate how one is to realize this life to the point where what is legislated is what drives one, rather than the free gift of grace and life.

So you have that tension between the law that gives structure, and in this case the law of love and freedom, and the actual freedom we have in Jesus Christ. So I am free in Christ. Apart from Jesus Christ and faith in him, I am in bondage. I'm enslaved. And so even then, when I claim I'm free and living apart from Jesus Christ, I'm actually living as a slave to sin, seeking life through created things, rather than life through faith in Jesus Christ.

Extravagant Grace

I like the use of the language of abundance, of extravagance over against the language of scarcity. I wrote a piece some time ago, which was published in the journal *Dialog* [*Dialog: A Journal of Theology*] in which I emphasized that God's grace is not scarce. If God's grace were scarce then we would have to be selective about who are the ones chosen to hear and receive the grace of God. But if God's grace is abundant, and God is extravagant about offering this grace, which comes in and through very concrete means—like water, like bread and wine, like the spoken word, like the act of graciousness and hospitality in the name of Jesus—if God's grace is extravagant, then to be other than extravagant in sharing it is to violate the very nature of God's self-giving. Let God's humor humor us that God would be so extravagant in sharing and making it available. Let that characterize our lives rather than watching the market on how well we are protecting God's grace.

If one daily remembers one's baptism, one is remembering, on the one hand, but for the grace of God I'm nothing. And simultaneously one is remembering, "Thanks be to God for Jesus' sake, and in the power of the Spirit, that this nobody is indeed somebody." And she or he—I—can lift our heads high and say, "I belong, I'm somebody, because of the one to whom I belong."

HOW TO RECEIVE COMMUNION

Foster R. McCurley

That is confusing to many people—why the sacrament is called by so many different names. But each one emphasizes something different. The title that I prefer is "the Lord's Supper," because that indeed is the sum total of the whole thing. It's how it began. It's what it looks forward to, and it's that in which we participate right now.

"Eucharist" is very frequently used for it. Eucharist is a Greek word that means "thanksgiving." And even in modern Greek today, if you want to say thank you, you say *Efharisto*, which is the same word—thank you.

The difficulty, I think, with simply using the word "Eucharist" for the sacrament is it emphasizes the thanksgiving that we offer, rather than the action of God that precedes it. So the Lord's Supper indicates more clearly, I think, that this is God's act. It's what the Lord instituted, what the Lord in fact commands us to do. And it involves that it's a supper given and prepared and offered freely to us.

"Communion" is another interesting word, because sometimes when we're receiving the sacrament, we tend to look at it as a kind of individual thing—that this is between God and *me*. The word "communion" means "fellowship." And therefore the "me" is involved with other "me's" and it's a whole family of sisters and brothers participating in this meal. So that is an important word too, except it's more our participation in it rather than God's action. So again, I always like to come back to the word the "Lord's Supper," which indicates who the subject of the whole thing is. Who's the actor, and who makes it occur?

Jesus indicates that the church that follows him—the disciples and all the rest, for years to come until that moment—are to celebrate the same Lord's Supper. As he indicates, you proclaim the Lord's death until he comes. So by proclaiming the Lord's death again and again and again and again, in this "meantime" period, it becomes the present reality for everyone who participates. "For you," Jesus said. "My body for you. My blood for you." It's always this wondrously present event even though it's past and it's future right now. Christ is present with us, offering the same gift he gave to his disciples in

A.D. 29, and the same one that will occur for all creation in the kingdom to come. That's the beauty, I think, of this particular sacrament. It has this wondrous, timeless quality about it. And we're always ever present. Not observers, but really participants, as receivers in this gift that Christ keeps giving.

Why Is It a Sacrament?

Luther defined the sacrament as "that which exists because God commanded it," on one hand, and because it expresses the fullness of God's will, which is freedom, forgiveness of sins, life, salvation—all at once, and really unambiguously.

It's God's, by God's command, and it is this wondrous gift of forgiveness with fringe benefits, if I may, of life and salvation. What makes it a sacrament too is it's solely God's act.

The best way we can receive the sacrament is by recognizing that it is solely God's act. The best way for me to come to the altar and there participate in the sacrament as a recipient is to be clear in my head that I am bringing nothing to this. I'm coming—to use Luther's words—as a beggar. I have nothing to offer. Just receive. And that's what God is accomplishing here—Christ once again is present and offering this wondrous amazing grace.

So a more proper attitude in receiving the sacrament would be, "Here I am, Lord. I bring nothing at all. Let me have it." And what you get is amazing grace—a wondrous, wondrous gift of forgiveness.

God's Word Comes to Us

I think we have difficulty talking about it because there is a sense that it is as mysterious as the Word of God becoming incarnate. How do we explain that? We don't really have the words to talk about something absolutely so unique. And so the same thing is true when it comes to the sacrament of the Lord's Supper. It is such a unique experience that it's hard to actually think of parallels. I can think of parallels for some parts of it, but not for the whole action. I can think of the fact that the sacrament of the Lord's Supper is one of the ways that God's word comes to us.

Luther said that God's word comes to us, is present with us, lays claim on us, comforts us in terms of the preaching of the word. It is what the preacher does on a Sunday morning in terms of the sacraments. The word comes to us in the words of absolution, your sins are forgiven. And the word comes to us, Luther said, in a mutual consolation of the sisters and brothers as one will comfort another in faith with the message of Christ.

And so that Word of God is coming in the sacrament in a very different way. The content is the same, but the mode is a bit different, now in the context of a meal. And so one can talk about this being a meal. It is kind of sparse, when you think about it, for our meal. Just a little taste of wine, which probably isn't all that good a vintage anyway. Just a piece of bread, whether that is an unleavened wafer (which is almost tasteless), or the gift that some member of the congregation made in the oven before church (which could be quite delicious). But that is just a foretaste of something to come.

Signs of Christ's Body and Blood

Does it have to be wine? There are circumstances where probably it should not be wine. There are people who cannot drink alcohol. And the effect of the sacrament is not dependent upon the alcoholic content of the beverage. There are many people and many congregations who use grape juice, sometimes for specific individuals and sometimes for the whole congregation. I think it's important that an option be made for people who cannot drink the wine. And that could be grape juice.

Could it be Coca-Cola® or Triscuits®? Under dire circumstances if nothing else is possible, nothing else is available, I would think it could be. Because what is really important in the sacrament are the words, "My body given for you. My blood shed for you." It's the sacrifice of the person of Christ that's being offered, in one sense in spite of whatever the menu might be. But in order to connect with that past, future, and present, it is again helpful, I think, for us to stay as close as we can to the way Jesus offered it.

The bread and the wine are symbols only when we understand that they are what they symbolize. And that is to say, they are meant in this sacrament to represent the gift of Christ's body. And so the bread can remain bread. The wine can remain wine, but again it's those words, "given for you, shed for you" that at that moment give them significance. It doesn't make them different. It doesn't change the chemistry of them. It just gives them the significance that God is at this moment using these very common ordinary things to be a vehicle through which the Word of God comes to us once again.

They're symbols of something beyond themselves—the bread and wine. But I'd almost prefer to use the word "signs." They are signs. They point to something other than themselves. And they point to that in the context of the Word.

Administering the Lord's Supper

We tend to use the pastor as the one who administers the sacrament of the Lord's Supper because, in Luther's understanding, that's for the sake of good order. And that is to say, because this understanding of the sacrament is different from, let's say, the Roman Catholic perspective on one hand, or the view of many Protestant churches on the other hand, where it is only a memorial. It is so different that part of Luther's understanding is the one who officiates at the sacrament ought to be the one who, at the same time, can explain what's happening here. This real presence of Christ forgiving us in the midst of the eating and drinking.

So from Luther's understanding, it's basically good order. It's why we have the Office of Ordination in the first place—for the sake of good order. Basically, I think that means that every baptized Christian is responsible to bear witness to the Word of God wherever he or she is. But the ordained pastor is *accountable* to do it according to the teachings of the church—not just responsible but accountable at the same time.

So the same thing is true, I think, then in administering the sacrament. It is this one who has the office we call of Word and Sacrament that is held accountable to do it according to the teachings of the church and to help the congregation understand what those teachings are.

Again, there are many places where it's important to have other members of the congregation, shall we say, *commissioned* to be lay communion assistants. And that might even mean not only assisting—usually with the wine (the cup at a worship service), but it also might mean commissioned to go out to the nursing homes, to private homes, to administer the sacrament there, to assist the pastor by being the carriers of the sacrament—the "proclaimers" of it in various situations.

If you have bread and wine left over from communion, what should you do with it? It's important to remember that it's still bread and it's still wine. Nothing magical has happened to it because of its role in the offering of the sacrament. Yet it probably is important, if not more so, than the food that we ask God to bless at a mealtime. It is food that we acknowledge that we receive. It's food we acknowledge to use in the service of God because God strengthens us through it. But, ultimately, it's still wine and it's still bread.

Now if I were drinking a glass of wine and there was some left over and I didn't want to drink any more, would I put it back into the bottle? Probably not. It wouldn't be a good way to keep wine. I think if there's wine left over, it probably should be—what should we say—respectfully disposed of.

If there's bread left over? If it's unleavened bread, well, then it can be left over for the next time. If it's a loaf that's been baked, it won't last till next time, and so someone probably ought to eat it. It was made for eating.

So what is to be done with it is always a question that I think has as much to do with Paul's admonition, "Do not offend the weaker brother or sister." [See 1 Corinthians 8 and 10:23-33.] Do not do anything with the leftover elements that would offend someone else in the congregation or anywhere else. But treat them with respect.

Why would a pastor withhold communion? Well, if I were the pastor, I would do that under only very exceptional circumstances because, again, the gift of the sacrament is for us as we are. And that's not always the way someone else would like us to be. And so it's very hard to indicate to someone they should not participate, should not receive the sacrament.

On the other hand, Luther does spend a good deal of time talking about the fact that if Christ is really present there—if the Word of God is present with us, then the Word can and is intended in this case to comfort the afflicted. But it might also afflict the comfortable. And that is to say, the presence of the Word of God—the presence of Christ among us might be judgment against someone who ridicules the sacrament who says, "This is a bunch of hogwash, but I'm going to go up and have my bread and wine anyway." There are attitudes that could exist that would almost cause—almost force—a pastor to say, "It might be better if you did not receive, as long as you are so arrogant against this gift of God and the way this means of grace works."

The Word of God that we receive in the sacrament is the same Word of God that we've received in a sermon, in our conversation together. And that Word always can have a judging edge (the law) or a saving edge (the gospel). And sometimes, because it's so personal, because it's the Word from God coming to address you and me, it can hit us different ways at different times.

Kids Eat Free

You know, every once in awhile there will be on a marquee at some restaurant, usually part of a big chain somewhere, that will say, "Kids eat free." There's a sense in which every church should announce that when the sacrament or the Lord's Supper is going to be celebrated on a Sunday morning : "Kids eat free." And that means to say, "All God's children eat free." It's once again this absolutely free, unconditional gift from God. This amazing grace that's given to us free of charge.

So what I get out of it is this constant gift. And with that gift of forgiveness comes a new lease on life. And with a new lease on life a whole new understanding of how when I go through the doors and exit into the world, I have just been dismissed to go in peace and serve the Lord. And interestingly, the response to that is, "Thanks be to God." It's a thanksgiving of joy and praise because we are set free, we are made new, and why wouldn't I want to receive that? It's what I get out of it. I give hardly anything, you see, except to proceed one foot in front of the other. (They usually walk up to the altar table and receive.) That's all I give. It's just being there with a faith that God has already given me to receive this wondrous grace.

THE THREE MOST REBELLIOUS THINGS JESUS DID

Barbara R. Rossing

What Lutherans emphasize is grace. Now, Jesus was not a Lutheran, of course. That's anachronistic. But he was God's gracious presence alive in the flesh in our world. So a Lutheran focus would be looking at how Jesus was fully human and gives us a window into the heart of God in all that he did, in the people that he ate with, in the people that he taught and ministered to—that this is how we see God's presence in our world, and it's a gracious presence. That would be the most important thing for a Lutheran emphasis, which is not to say that other denominations don't emphasize grace also. They do. But I think this is really our Lutheran vocation, to focus on the gracious presence of God in Jesus and to look at how Jesus taught us a way of life that is full of God's grace. And Jesus teaches us how to see God's grace in our world.

Another Lutheran dimension, I think, is the humor and the whimsical presence of Jesus. He didn't do a lot of discussing doctrine, but he told stories. And I think we can really pick up on that as Lutherans as well. The way we embody God's presence isn't just in abstract teaching so much as in down-to-earth storytelling and living the stories in our relationships with one another. And that's how we see the presence of Jesus in our world. That's a Lutheran understanding—that he's fully human and a great storyteller.

Jesus' Life and Ministry

His baptism was also his ordination. That was the beginning then of his ministry, the beginning of his public ministry. And I like to point that out to students, because it's baptism that ordains us. And Jesus was never ordained as a pastor. He was baptized. All of us have that same kind of ordination that sets us then in ministry to the world. And that began Jesus' public ministry where he then starts right out with healing. And it's an exorcism so it's this driving out of demons, which I think is emblematic of how he basically thought that the world was possessed, whether by Roman power, by demonic power, by everything. And he begins then to cast out these demons that had been holding people captive in all kinds of ways.

He gathers disciples. He calls people to join him in this movement and they do—that's the amazing thing. They drop everything and they follow him and they join up. He calls people. Then he also enacts the kingdom by these amazing feedings that he does, where he is not afraid to say there is enough. God's world is one of abundance. It looks like there's only five loaves and a couple of fishes. But God can take these—what look like limited resources—and God can make enough.

So in everything that Jesus did he's showing people God's way of life, which is this vision of healing and renewal for the world. That when people were suffering under—well, we know that Herod the Great imposed even worse taxation and worse oppressive measures than previously had been the case, when Herod the Great was a puppet king for the Romans. And people were really suffering. They were losing their land. They were going further and further into debt, so they were becoming debt slaves. And things looked really hopeless.

Moreover, it was a very violent time. The Romans would regularly crucify people who wouldn't fall into the plan. Anybody who was a threat would get crucified—not just Jesus. They had crucified whole villages. And into this hopeless-looking situation, Jesus comes with this message of hope and renewal and shows people that God hasn't given up on the world. That the way of life that was inaugurated in the Old Testament of manna and a vision, of enough for all, of God caring for little people, of renewing village life—this was still happening even though it might be hard to see. And Jesus helps people get the eyes to see what God is doing in the world. And he challenges the systems of oppression with a different vision of God's work in the world.

He walked from village to village. We do not know if he fished himself, but he certainly worked with fishermen who were making their livelihood on the Sea of Galilee. He could go out in boats with them. He told stories about fish, and he told many, many stories about farming. So he seems to have known the peasant way of life intimately and uses the image of casting seeds, for example, as God is the abundant sower who strew seeds everywhere. And people would have understood this parable and would have known the way of life he was talking about. So that was where Jesus' life centered until he made the decision to go to Jerusalem and confront the authorities there. Otherwise, he was rural and he went from village to village and preached and taught. He did venture north up into the area that was known as Phoenicia, Caesarea Philippi. But he didn't travel far. It's a small area and very rural.

A Way of Life

He seems to have looked for the outcast, for the woman with a daughter who needed healing. He was able to go mix also with Gentiles, with Romans, soldiers, we think. We do not know, all we have are the stories in the gospels. But he seems to have been somebody who did surprising things. And if you go with the Gospel of Luke, he was somebody who loved to eat. One scholar has pointed out that in every chapter of Luke, there's something about eating. It's a little bit of a stretch. You have to say that when Jesus is laid in a manger in Luke chapter 2 that that little manger is a feed box. So that's where the animals get their food. So if you count that, there's feeding or eating or talk about food in every chapter of Luke's Gospel. So he seems to have loved to eat.

So I think that when we fixate on the element of the supernatural and think that that's what makes a miracle a miracle. Jesus, by the way, wasn't the only one who did those things. I remember when I was traveling in the Middle East and traveling in Greece and Turkey and learning about other healers at the time of Jesus or others who did these things. That's not what makes Jesus unique. What makes Jesus unique is his servanthood way of life, and his servanthood even to the point of being crucified and inviting us to follow him in that way of life. I think that's quite unprecedented in Roman occupation times in the ancient world.

I think when we think that the only message of Jesus is that he came to die for your sins and to take you to heaven, that we're missing something. If we narrow the message of Jesus down to just that—atonement—it misses the whole way of life that Jesus teaches us. The eating with sinners and tax collectors, the preaching a gospel of peace, the Sermon on the Mount, the whole way of life that Jesus inaugurated as he went about in Galilee and then undertook his journey to Jerusalem. All along the way he was healing the world. He was teaching people. He was giving hope. Certainly, Jesus came to die for our sins and to take us to heaven. But that's not the core message of the gospel. It's so much more than that. It's a way of seeing our world in the heart of God that Jesus teaches. And he opens up God's heart to us. So, Lutherans sometimes tend to miss that, by focusing so much just on sin and then the forgiveness of sins. We need the whole message of the Gospel.

Jesus and You

What does Jesus have to do with my life? Everything. And I hope that the viewers of this will agree with that—that the more you get to know Jesus in the scriptures, the more you read the stories about him and get to know him in your life, the more central he becomes. He's wonderfully irresistible, and I think we really need to unabashedly say that as Lutherans. That this is the person who changed the world and continues to change our world and each of our lives and has a wonderful power for love and for grace—that is the anchor for everything that we're about.

So, yes, to say that Jesus is everything to me—I mean it sounds pious—but I think that that's what our hymns teach us. That's what the scriptures teach us. Following Jesus is at the heart of what we are called to be about as God's people.

No, I'm a pietist, but I'm also one who believes in social justice, and those two go together. I think the more deeply we understand Jesus as being in our heart and in our spirit the more deeply we understand the call to follow Jesus into the world and to love the world that he also loved.

My friend, Dan Erlander, a pastor, has a wonderful cartoon of a man who is praying to Jesus. [See cartoon on p. 49 in this book and on p. 25 in the Workbook.] And Jesus is there, but he's also surrounded by poor people and outcasts and disabled people and women and prostitutes and sinners and tax collectors. And the guy is praying to Jesus and he says, "Lord, why is it that every time I pray that you will come into my heart, you bring all your friends with you?" And I think that's a great cartoon. That's how it is. When we invite Jesus into our heart, then we are inviting all his friends with him. He's going to bring the whole world and that's what it means to have Jesus in your heart.

I think it also means a kind of reversal of that as well. And this would be where a Lutheran understanding is really important, that Jesus invites us into God's heart. It's not that we put Jesus into my own personal heart. It's that Jesus, through our baptism, through the sacraments, brings us into God's heart and into the whole world. So it's an opening up of our heart.

Jesus is an icon of the presence of God. He opens his heart to show us God's heart and the heart of the world, which is the presence of God. So it's not just that I possess Jesus and I have him in my heart. It's much bigger than that. And even when you try for that, he's going to bring his friends with you into your heart, and before you know it you're going to be loving those other people as well. He doesn't come alone. He brings his friends.

The Unpopular Jesus

But not everybody wanted to be part of it. There are people who turn away—the rich man in Mark, chapter 10. He comes to Jesus with this question, "What must I do to inherit eternal life?" I think it's a healing story. I'm reading that story now as another story of healing because he falls down on his knees, just like the others who come to Jesus for healing. And it's this wonderful moment where Jesus, well, first Jesus says, well, you know, the commandments: Love God. Love your neighbor. Yes, yes, the man says. I've kept these for my whole life. And Jesus looks at him and loves him. And I think Jesus looks at us and loves all of us. But still the rich man can't take the cure that Jesus is offering. Jesus then says to him, "Go sell all that you have and give it to the poor and come and follow me." Jesus says that because he loves him. "Doctor" Jesus is trying to heal this man. And I think we need to hear that word today as well.

Doctor Jesus is trying to heal our *affluenza*. This is a term coined by a Seattle filmmaker named John De Graaf [producer of PBS documentaries *Affluenza* (1996) and *Escape from Affluenza* (1998) and author of *Affluenza: The All-Consuming Epidemic* with David Wann and Thomas H. Naylor (Berrett-Koehler Publishers, 2001)]. It's a combination of "affluence" and "influenza." I think our lifestyle is making us sick. It's making our world sick. We need to be cured of it. And Jesus looks at us so lovingly and says, "Here's the cure." But the question always is, will we take it? Can we take it? And the sadness in the Mark 10 story is that this guy has looked straight into the eyes of Jesus. He's seen Jesus' love. And not very many other stories have that same phrase—Jesus looking at him, loves him. And still the guy turns away and goes sad, all by himself. He comes to Jesus alone. He could have been part of this amazing community, this renewal movement, and he goes away alone—he turns away.

And that's the temptation for all of us, to not want to be part of this vision for the kingdom. It's a hard message in some ways, but it's where we'll find true community. It's where we'll find true love. It's where we find all of our desires most deeply satisfied, but not everyone wants that. And the rich man very sadly goes away. I mean, I don't like to think that he goes away forever. He might have gotten it later. We do not know. There are so many stories in the Gospels that are left open-ended.

It's we who have watered Jesus down, I think. The Jesus of the Gospels is a Jesus who caused offense to the Roman authorities and to the religious and political elites of his own day. And I think that if we really see them as the message of the Gospel, it's equally troubling for us as well. So, I mean, people in Jesus' day had problems with who he was eating with, who he was forgiving, how welcoming and all-embracing he was, and how he didn't seem to support strong moral values in the way they wanted to, and they found him a threat.

They also found threatening the way he was going through the villages of Galilee, which were downtrodden under the increasing system of Rome and occupation and oppression. And Jesus was preaching a gospel of a kingdom—a different kingdom—which was threatening to Roman authorities, and I think in some ways it's threatening to us today too. So if we find Jesus easy and acceptable it's because we've made him over in our own image. I think the Jesus of the Bible is a challenging one to any generation, including our own. And that's the rebellious side and it's the wonderful side that we really need to hear—his critique of culture, his critique of empire. The way he extends himself to heal our world, to give a message of hope to people who had been taught that there is no hope for them because they are left out of the economy. They're the castaways, the downtrodden. And Jesus lifted them up and said, no, you are precious to God. You have a place in the world system, in a globalized economy. And what you are about and your life really matters to me. And I think we would find that message just as challenging today.

Yes, I think Jesus—the vision of what he offers—jumps off the pages of the Bible. It's captivating. This is a vision that our world really needs. And it's still as lively as it ever was. This is the heart of God and it's a vision that we need to follow and that is more inviting than all the other things that advertising teaches us to desire. It's a way of life that we really need—especially this vision of community.

HOW TO READ THE BIBLE

Rolf A. Jacobson

There was an old camp song that's not particularly Lutheran:

"B-I-B-L-E, Yes, that's the book for me . . ."

So the Bible is a book, but actually it's not a book. The Bible is a library. The Bible has sixty-six books in it, and it has two halves, although the halves are not equal in length or in terms of time.

The Bible Is Like a Newspaper

When you think about the Bible, one of the things to think about is that it's not a book in the sense of having only one kind of literature. Like a library it has many kinds of literature. And I think a good example of that is a newspaper. When you come to a newspaper, there's many different types of stories and different types of articles. There's fact articles that describe what happened. There's also editorials—opinions—what one person thinks about something. There's comics, which talk about truth, but they don't talk about truth in the same way that a story talks about truth. There are ads, there are advice columnists, and so on.

What that means is that you have to read each part of the newspaper differently. And just think to yourself, when you read a newspaper you're mentally adjusting as you go through each part of the newspaper. And we do that when we read the Bible too. We mentally adjust. So the Bible has different types of books and literature. It has poems, it has songs, it has proverbs, it has parables, it has historical books, it has letters, it has a love song, and it has prophetic messages.

So what is the Bible? It's a library with lots of different types of literature. What ties them all together is the common theme of God and what God is doing in the world today. And what ties them all together is that they are all relevant for our faith now.

Reading the Bible

❶ *Literally or figuratively?*

One of the big misconceptions about reading the Bible that I find people have is that people ask this, "Do you read the Bible literally, or do you read the Bible figuratively?" And I think that's a false question, as if people always read the Bible literally or always read the Bible figuratively.

Let me go back to my newspaper example again. Do you read the newspaper literally, or do you read it figuratively? When you're reading a news story you read it literally.

Here's a story about mercury in the environment. You'd read that story mostly literally, but then if you'd turn to the comics—my favorite comic is Dilbert. Do I read Dilbert literally? No. Dilbert's about the work environment, and it's got these characters that are like people you know—like the guy in Dilbert who walks around all day long with his coffee cup and never does any work. We all know somebody a little bit like that.

So, do you read that literally? No. You read that figuratively. You have to adjust when you're reading the newspaper, and you have to do the same thing in the Bible.

❷ *Law and gospel*

One of the things that happens is we can be reading a Bible passage together and you might hear it as a promise and I might hear it as a demand because the Spirit is working directly on our hearts. Well, that's the whole thing. You can't say, "Here's all the laws, here are all the gospel passages," and keep them forever separate, because the Word speaks to us and that's why the authority of the Bible is always what it's doing to us and the claim it's making on our lives.

Here's what's different about Lutherans. When we read the Bible, we read the Bible through the lens of justification by grace through faith. And we look for law and gospel in the Bible. So when we come to a passage, we are distinguishing between law and gospel.

The law says, "This is what you are to do and this is not a means to salvation." The gospel says, "This is what you cannot do. Only God can and will do this for you." And where we get mixed up is when we switch the two around.

Lutherans—what makes us different is the way in which we interpret the Bible and the way we interpret reality through justification with the idea of law and gospel.

The Authority of the Bible

There's different ways that Christians have thought about the authority of the Bible. And if you open up the Bible, you could imagine, some people think that the authority of the Bible comes from what's behind it—that is, from how it was written or from who wrote it. And so some people will say Moses wrote the first five books of the Bible—the Pentateuch. Other people will say when the Bible was written, it was inspired verbally—verbal inspiration. Which means God told somebody what to say and they said it. God told the hand what to write and they wrote it. That's sort of a behind-the-Bible view of inspiration and authority. Lutherans have never had that view, if we pay attention to Luther and how Lutherans have always read the Bible.

Rather, the authority of the Bible comes from what happens when the Bible preaches to me. It comes from the claims that the Bible makes on my life. When the Bible says to me, I am a sinner. When the Bible says to me, I am a child of God. When the Bible says to me, I am forgiven and I have a permanent relationship with God that I can't do anything about. And when that testimony takes hold in my life, that's where the authority of the Bible comes from. That's more of an in-front-of-the-Bible way of thinking about the authority of the Bible, and that's the traditional Lutheran view.

If I close the Bible and I put it on my bookshelf where it looks good with its gold embossed lettering on its leather binding, that's no longer the Word of God for me. It's the Word of God, but it's sort of frozen, like steaks in your freezer, which aren't really food until you eat them. It's the Word of God but it's not for me.

Luther had a great image that the Bible is like a cradle that holds the Christ child. And we come to it to find Jesus just as the Wise Men came to the cradle to find the baby Jesus.

Hurdles in Reading the Bible

❶ *Cultural distance*

The Bible can be intimidating as can any book. There's a couple of reasons for feeling intimidated or for the strangeness, or there's a couple of hurdles that you have to get over.

The first hurdle or the first challenge in reading the Bible is that it comes from a different culture in a different time. Its experience is so much different than mine. So it talks of God like a shepherd. Well, I've never met a shepherd and I don't plan on meeting any shepherd soon, because we don't have shepherds in America right now. Even our dairy and our sheep farmers aren't shepherds in the same way as in the Bible. But for the Old Testament that's the fundamental metaphor—one of the fundamental metaphors for God. And here's a secret about it. That's because in the Old Testament times, the fundamental picture of what a good king was, was that a good king was a shepherd. So when the Old Testament said God is like a shepherd, it was pulling something that everybody would have understood was an image for the king.

❷ *Assumption that the Bible is for experts*

A second problem with interpreting the Bible is that we've made the mistake, I think, at times of assuming that the Bible is a book for experts and you have to go to school in order to read the Bible. And so we let other people tell us what it means all the time, and that's an extreme. In the extreme, that's a mistake we want to get over. We don't want to go to the other extreme saying, "Well, I'm just going to read the Bible by myself and whatever I think is right."

❸ *Contradictions?*

I want to say, first of all, that the Bible is consistent about almost everything it says. Especially the Bible is consistent when it is talking about the one God who created everything that exists, and the one Savior who redeems us.

But there are places where the Bible seems to contradict itself. An example might be that you might read a passage where God says, "I'm going to condemn you for your sins and I will not save you." And then you read the majority of the passages, which talk about how God forgives sins and saves us.

In those cases what you'll find is that, where God says, "I'm going to condemn you for your sins," God is talking about a specific action, a specific time. So that passage is located tightly in history, usually in the Old Testament, whereas the other message is a universal message. So what you want to do is look at the context of the different passages that seem to contradict each other. And you might find that one is a message for a specific time and place, that we can learn from by analogy, whereas the other one is a universal message that applies everywhere.

Let me give you an example. My mom said to me once when I was a kid, "Don't cross the street!" Now, that was a message for that day and that hour. If I had interpreted that as a message for all of the universe, I would still be stuck on the 800 block of Sherman Avenue in Jackson, Minnesota, right? If I'd apply that forever I'm never allowed to cross the street.

Some of God's commandments are like that. God says, "Don't do this right now" or "I'm going to do this right now." They are not intended to be universal prohibitions.

❹ *Language*

The problem with language—George Carlin used to say, "The problem with those 'foreigners' is they have a different word for everything." The problem, of course, is that's not true. Some foreign languages might have six words for one of ours. And other languages might have one word for which we have no word. So in the Old Testament we have the concept of *ḥesed* and there's no English equivalent. Likewise, in English we have the word "love," but in the Greek of the New Testament times, there were at least four words for love. And so how do you translate that? Plus language is always changing. I have a daughter and she uses new words around the house and I have to ask what she means—and she's only six years old.

Using the Bible

After we first understand that the question to ask when we read the Bible is "What does this mean?" now how do we use it?

I need to start by saying how we should not use it. We should not use the Bible to try to score points in arguments, or to try to silence somebody whose viewpoint is different than ours. This is a big temptation.

It doesn't mean that the Bible can't help us wrestle with difficult issues, especially moral issues. But many of the moral issues we're facing today were not relevant in the culture two and a half thousand years ago.

❶ *In worship*

So how do we read the Bible? I want to start with when Christians come together. The first way to read the Bible is to go to worship. We read the Bible together in worship. In our official lectionary, we have four readings. We have an Old Testament reading, a Psalm, a New Testament epistle reading, and then a reading from one of the four Gospels, and then a sermon, which is usually based on one or more of those four lessons. So that's a way to read the Bible. We go, the Bible is read to us, and somebody preaches about one of those passages.

Also at worship what happens is we sing and we pray the Bible. So most of the songs that we have are singing the Bible.

❷ *In groups*

I think that coming together is a great way to read the Bible, that we should be reading the Bible in groups. Even if we don't have experts present (and I think it's great not to have experts present, even though I am by profession a Bible expert), we come together and we agree to discuss the Bible. So that's a great way to read the Bible—to read it in groups of four people, six people. It doesn't have to be official. You don't have to get the church's blessing. You can have your neighbors over and do it.

❸ *Just start*

You don't have to sit down for an hour and put out, you know, rolls and a cup of coffee to have a Bible study. It can take five minutes there in the morning as you're trying to get kids out the door. The key thing is to start.

My grandpa sent eight kids to St. Olaf College. And somebody asked him, "How do you send eight kids to college? How do you pay for that?" And he said, "You start." And that's how you read the Bible. You just start.

HOW TO SHARE YOUR FAITH WITH SOMEONE

Kelly A. Fryer

I don't think it's possible to understand evangelism, or evangelizing, or being evangelical people, apart from God's mission in the world. These two things are connected. It's not possible to separate them out. We know from the stories in the Bible that God is on a mission to love and bless and save the whole world. That's what God is up to. The point of all this isn't the church. The point is the world, and the God we know through Jesus who is madly in love with the world.

To be the church is to be the people who have been called out by God to participate in that mission. That's what it means to be the church—to be people who know that we've been called on this mission to let God use us to bless the whole world. We can't understand what it means to be the church apart from that. The church doesn't have any mission except that mission—to be a part of what God is up to in the world—loving and blessing and saving everybody. That's what it means to be the church.

So evangelizing is at the very center of what that means. To be an evangelical people—that's at the very heart of what it means to be a church. It isn't one of the things in a smorgasbord of things that defines us. To be the church is to be an evangelical people, to be the people through whom God brings Jesus to the world.

Have You Met Jesus?

I'm not exactly sure how to say this in a way that doesn't sound harsh, but I wonder if we're not very good at evangelism because we're not exactly really clear about the fact that we've been met by Jesus. I think that it just might be a faith issue.

There's something about being met by Jesus that changes your life and makes you want to share that with everybody. So it begs the question, if we're not sharing that with everybody, have we been met by Jesus?

What happens when the word is proclaimed? Jesus comes. What happens when the sacrament of baptism is shared? Jesus comes. What happens when we receive communion? We receive Jesus. This is an evangelical event. Have you met Jesus? Well, did you hear the word today? Did you receive this bread, this wine? Is the body and blood of Jesus Christ given for you? You were met by Jesus—meaning, it's not like we have to go racing around the world looking for Jesus. Jesus comes to us! Jesus comes to us. You know, there's that simple image, right, of an arrow that comes down. God always comes down. God comes down in the bread and the wine. God comes down in the water of baptism. God comes down in the word that's spoken. God comes down in the community that we share as Christians. God came down in Jesus. God comes down in Jesus. God always comes down. There's never anything that we could do to flip that arrow around and make our way *up* to God. It's a gift. So, have you met Jesus? Have you been met by Jesus? Yes.

The Gift Is a Call

At the heart of Lutheran theology is this wonderful idea that we're saved by grace through faith apart from any works that we do, any works of the law. And I think that too often that's translated by Lutherans as being this—I'm saved as a gift, and so therefore I don't have to do anything. And we separate out—again I think without meaning to—but we separate out this wonderful gift of God's grace through Jesus Christ. We separate out the gift of salvation from the call to discipleship. We separate out the gift of salvation from the call to follow Jesus. When Jesus came up to Levi at the tax-collecting booth, he didn't say, "Levi, I love you." Or, "Levi, you're so saved." He said, "Levi, come follow me." Now Levi didn't do anything to deserve that. It was a gift, but the gift was a call, and I think we separate those two things out. And so I think it might be that in lots of our congregations—and again I don't know how to say this without sounding harsh—but I think in many of our congregations there may be people who have heard I'm saved as a gift and so therefore I don't have to do anything. And that would include sharing our faith.

In his little book, *The Freedom of a Christian*, Martin Luther talks about the freedom that is ours in Christ. As a gift, through Jesus Christ—through faith in Jesus Christ—we are set free from sin, death, and the devil, and anything else that would mess our lives up if it could. We are free as a gift. At the same time, he says—and he actually puts these two sentences right next to each other—we're set free from all that stuff for service to our neighbor. This is a Lutheran paradox, and I think it's a wonderful contribution to the conversation about evangelism. You can't separate out freedom. You can't separate out the gift from the call. These two things have to be held in tension.

Stop Thinking Church

People always ask me this question—they might not always use exactly these words, but this is what's behind the question. The question always is this, "Kelly, how can we save our church?" That's the question. "How can we save our church? You know, our church is in trouble. We don't have as many people as we used to. We don't have as much money. There aren't any young people. How could we save our church? Can we save our church?"

I always try to help folks in as kind and gentle a way as I am capable of. But here's a confession. Here's what I'm thinking in the back of my mind. What I'm thinking is here is how you save your church: Stop thinking so much about your church. That's what I really want to say. Stop thinking so much about your church. Your church is not the point. The point is this world that we live in that God loves so much. The point is the person who lives next door to you, or sits in the cube next to you, or fixes your car, or does your hair—he, she, they, are the point. And as long as we are focused on "our church," we're going to just continue to be in a big mess. God is on a mission to save that person who does your hair, that person who is sitting in the cube next to you. God wants those people to know what you know—that you're loved.

I think an evangelizing congregation looks a lot like an evangelizing person except there are more of us. You know, an evangelizing congregation is going to be a congregation that knows that it is not the be-all and end-all, that, in fact, it exists not for the sake of the people who are in it. An evangelizing congregation knows that it exists for the sake of people who aren't in it yet. That's what it means to be the church.

Maybe one of the first things that we should do is stop using the word "evangelism" as though it's a noun, or a program, or a thing that you do. It also just scares people too much. I don't know what the alternative word would be.

Some friends of mine and I have a new book out called *The Evangelizing Church* (Augsburg Fortress, 2005). And we propose instead of using the word "evangelism" we talk about being an evangelizing people. It's more of a verb or an adverb. It's about who we are, not about what we do. I don't know if that makes any sense. It's maybe a minor distinction, but evangelism—we too easily separate it off and we make it a program of the church. We make it the job of a particular committee. And as long as we've asked somebody over there to do it, then we don't have to be responsible for it. And it seems to me, if we're Christians, if we're people who've answered the call to follow Jesus, then we are by virtue of that identity an evangelizing people.

Seeing People

The best evangelist I've ever known was a woman who was a member of one of the congregations that I served as pastor. She worked in a salon and she is one of the shyest people I've ever known—very reserved, very shy. If you meet her in a crowd, she's the person standing back on the wall. She was responsible for bringing more people to that congregation than anybody else. And it was remarkable. She worked with them at the salon, or her neighbors, or the parents of kids who played on ball teams with their kids. And it was astounding how many people could trace their coming to that congregation to her.

And she would always say, when asked, that the reason she invited so many people to come to church is because she loved her church. She probably did love her church. But here's the real truth—she loved people. And she saw them. When she was talking to them she could see them. She could see the emptiness. She could see the difficulty. She could see how much they needed what she had found and it was the most natural thing in the world for her to invite those people to come.

I think, you know, there are a variety of things that I could say in response to the question, "How do we kind of get over ourselves in order to become more evangelical?" It might start here. It might start with just loving our neighbors. And that might start with just looking at them—just daring to look at them and to see who they really are.

There was a woman who joined the congregation that I served as pastor right after we opened our new ministry center. And she had been so disconnected from the church through her whole adult life.

She'd been married in the church, but no connection after that. In fact, her adult children hadn't been baptized and none of her grandchildren had been baptized.

Anyway, she told me that after she started coming to worship and joined the congregation, it was the most natural thing in the world for her to be talking to everyone about what she was experiencing. And all of a sudden, everyone that she worked with started talking about their church activities and what they had done that weekend at their congregation. And she told me that she never said this to them, because she didn't want to hurt their feelings. But she said to me, "I went through such terrible times in my life working right alongside all these people, and never did any of them invite me to come to church with them, or talk to me about their faith, or offer to pray with me, or even offer to pray *for* me. None of them dared to talk about those things, until I started talking about how I was going to church." And she said, "I just keep asking myself, now why didn't they share that with me? It could have made such a difference."

SMALL GROUP LEADER'S GUIDE

There Is NO "Right" Answer

Thank you for being a small group leader for The Lutheran Course. Your role is vital to the success of the course, but it does not require theological training or biblical expertise. In fact, there is only one thing you need to remember in order to do it right: There is no right answer. Say it again, out loud: There is NO "Right" Answer. Again, with conviction: *There is NO "Right" Answer.*

Your job here is to generate discussion. There is no doctrine that you must impart, no central truth that you must get across, no special knowledge you must share with your group. The task before you is simply to start a conversation, try to keep it going, and try to make sure that everyone has a chance to speak.

Not everyone in your group will be in the same place in their thinking. Even for some life-long Lutherans some of the ideas in *The Lutheran Handbook* and The Lutheran Course may seem new and foreign. The object is not to get everyone to agree, but to get people talking, sharing, and thinking. No question is too "stupid," no idea is too "outlandish," no one's opinion is "wrong." (OK, if someone in your group begins to suggest burning heretics at the stake, you may want to correct that. Burning at the stake went out of style some time ago, and the fact that there is no right answer means there are no heretical answers, either. So you may want to step in on that one.) But otherwise, your role is to encourage everyone to speak their mind and express their opinions in a group that is safe, accepting, and willing to listen, even if not everyone agrees.

Let's Talk

You'll want to spend some time in each session just chatting so that group members get to know one another. This is not wasted time. This helps the group get to know one another and feel comfortable in one another's company. It will be easier for people to talk openly about matters of faith if they are among friends they trust. A bit of time in each session to simply share joys and sorrows that have occurred since the last meeting is to be encouraged. The group will want to include the most significant of these joys and sorrows in a group prayer, perhaps immediately, or perhaps just before the session concludes—do as you feel is right. Don't feel that you, as leader, must always be in charge of these prayers. You can certainly invite others to take turns at different meetings, or ask all to offer portions of the prayer around the circle. Again, you'll sense what is right for your group.

A Small Group Covenant is provided in the workbook (p. 36), so that everyone in the group can agree on some clear expectations. It would be good, at the first meeting, to talk about these expectations and to ask group members to make this covenant, or contract, with one another. Basic expectations should include regular participation by all, openness and respect for the opinions of others even if all cannot accept or agree with them, and perhaps most importantly, group confidentiality.

What happens in the group should stay in the group. Participants will feel more free to share their thoughts and feelings if they have some assurance

The Lutheran Course Leader Book, copyright © 2005 Augsburg Fortress.
May be reproduced for local use.

these won't be topics of discussion tomorrow at the local coffee shop. If someone shares something you feel needs some action or intervention, talk to your pastor about it. He or she has been trained about keeping confidences.

The Workbook Was Made for You
There are two sets of pages in the workbook for each of the seven sessions. One set of workbook pages is designed for use in the large group setting immediately after viewing the video. The second set of workbook pages is for you to use in the small group. The activities, videos, and workbook pages used in the large group session are primarily designed to get people thinking about new things they will want to talk about in the small group. These will be the jumping off point for your discussion.

The workbook pages provided for the small group are tools that you may use to help generate more conversation in your group. You will not need every tool in the toolbox, nor should you feel that you must complete everything there. If one or two items launch enough talk for the entire time you are together, don't feel that you've failed because you didn't get all the exercises finished. Actually, you've succeeded splendidly because you accomplished the primary goal of creating a discussion and still had tools left over. Pick and choose the portions of the small group workbook exercises that you feel will work best in your group—some of them, all of them, or if you have some other way to get the conversation started, none of them at all. To paraphrase Mark 2:27, the workbook was made for you, not you for the workbook!

Twisting Arms
While you want to encourage everyone to take part in the conversation, some people are more naturally shy than others. Some will speak right up, others will need time to warm up to the group and to the idea of a discussion in which all questions and ideas are welcome. Don't twist anyone's arm. Part of creating a safe and inviting arena in which to speak is giving everyone the right to "pass" if they don't feel like speaking at the moment. This may make your job a bit more difficult in the beginning, but it will pay dividends later on.

Most of all, have fun. Enjoy getting to know the others in your group and becoming a participant along with them. As the group grows more comfortable, and learns the routine and the safe ground rules you've established, they will be more likely to become "self-starting" and will depend on you less and less. This is a good thing. It means you've done your job well. Then you'll be able to just settle in and enjoy being just another group member. You'll know you're finished when you've worked yourself out of a job, and the group begins to jump into conversation, prayer, and serious discussion with very little help from you. Of course, they still may need someone to watch the clock or keep things moving along, but getting things started will be much less difficult.

What Am I Getting Into Here?
At the end of the seventh and final session of The Lutheran Course, each small group is asked to consider its future. Some of these groups will choose simply to disband. Others will have come to value one another and their time together and will want to continue to meet even after The Lutheran Course has ended. You'll have just as much say in that as anyone else in the group. But your commitment is for the seven sessions of this course. Any commitments to ongoing meetings will need to be decided later, and there is no automatic assumption that you'll continue meeting, that you would continue to be in a leadership role, or that you are supposed to steer the group toward a particular decision. There are no hidden expectations here. Wait and see what happens and decide then what you wish your role to be, if any.

If your small group does continue, your pastor will be able to suggest some possible resources that your group might use for ongoing discussion.

Again, thank you for being a small group discussion leader for The Lutheran Course.

The Lutheran Course Leader Book, copyright © 2005 Augsburg Fortress.
May be reproduced for local use.

IN WHAT WAY CAN YOU HEAR LAW AND GOSPEL IN EACH OF THESE PASSAGES?

Genesis 12:1-3
Now the Lord said to Abram, "Go from your country and your kindred and your father's house to the land that I will show you. ²I will make of you a great nation, and I will bless you, and make your name great, so that you will be a blessing. ³I will bless those who bless you, and the one who curses you I will curse; and in you all the families of the earth shall be blessed."

Exodus 20:2-3
²I am the Lord your God, who brought you out of the land of Egypt, out of the house of slavery; ³you shall have no other gods before me.

Jeremiah 31:31-34
³¹The days are surely coming, says the Lord, when I will make a new covenant with the house of Israel and the house of Judah. ³²It will not be like the covenant that I made with their ancestors when I took them by the hand to bring them out of the land of Egypt — a covenant that they broke, though I was their husband, says the Lord. ³³But this is the covenant that I will make with the house of Israel after those days, says the Lord: I will put my law within them, and I will write it on their hearts; and I will be their God, and they shall be my people. ³⁴No longer shall they teach one another, or say to each other, "Know the Lord," for they shall all know me, from the least of them to the greatest, says the Lord; for I will forgive their iniquity, and remember their sin no more.

Matthew 9:1-13
And after getting into a boat he crossed the sea and came to his own town.

²And just then some people were carrying a paralyzed man lying on a bed. When Jesus saw their faith, he said to the paralytic, "Take heart, son; your sins are forgiven." ³Then some of the scribes said to themselves, "This man is blaspheming." ⁴But Jesus, perceiving their thoughts, said, "Why do you think evil in your hearts? ⁵For which is easier, to say, 'Your sins are forgiven,' or to say, 'Stand up and walk'? ⁶But so that you may know that the Son of Man has authority on earth to forgive sins" — he then said to the paralytic — "Stand up, take your bed and go to your home." ⁷And he stood up and went to his home. ⁸When the crowds saw it, they were filled with awe, and they glorified God, who had given such authority to human beings.

⁹As Jesus was walking along, he saw a man called Matthew sitting at the tax booth; and he said to him, "Follow me." And he got up and followed him.

¹⁰And as he sat at dinner in the house, many tax collectors and sinners came and were sitting with him and his disciples. ¹¹When the Pharisees saw this, they said to his disciples, "Why does your teacher eat with tax collectors and sinners?" ¹²But when he heard this, he said, "Those who are well have no need of a physician, but those who are sick. ¹³Go and learn what this means, 'I desire mercy, not sacrifice.' For I have come to call not the righteous but sinners."

John 14:6 and 14:15
⁶Jesus said to him, "I am the way, and the truth, and the life. No one comes to the Father except through me."
¹⁵"If you love me, you will keep my commandments."

Acts 2:37-39
³⁷Now when they heard this, they were cut to the heart and said to Peter and to the other apostles, "Brothers, what should we do?" ³⁸Peter said to them, "Repent, and be baptized every one of you in the name of Jesus Christ so that your sins may be forgiven; and you will receive the gift of the Holy Spirit. ³⁹For the promise is for you, for your children, and for all who are far away, everyone whom the Lord our God calls to him."

Romans 12:1-2
I appeal to you therefore, brothers and sisters, by the mercies of God, to present your bodies as a living sacrifice, holy and acceptable to God, which is your spiritual worship. ²Do not be conformed to this world, but be transformed by the renewing of your minds, so that you may discern what is the will of God — what is good and acceptable and perfect.

Revelation 21:22-27
²²I saw no temple in the city, for its temple is the Lord God the Almighty and the Lamb. ²³And the city has no need of sun or moon to shine on it, for the glory of God is its light, and its lamp is the Lamb. ²⁴The nations will walk by its light, and the kings of the earth will bring their glory into it. ²⁵Its gates will never be shut by day and there will be no night there. ²⁶People will bring into it the glory and the honor of the nations. ²⁷But nothing unclean will enter it, nor anyone who practices abomination or falsehood, but only those who are written in the Lamb's book of life.

Session 1: Photocopy for use in the large group.
The Lutheran Course Leader Book, copyright © 2005 Augsburg Fortress. May be reproduced for local use.
Scripture quotations are from *New Revised Standard Version Bible*, copyright © 1989 Division of Christian Education of the National Council of the Churches of Christ in the United States of America. Used by permission.

TABLE TALK

When you hear the word, "Lutheran," what's the first thing that comes to mind?

TABLE TALK

When you hear the word, "Lutheran," what's the first thing that comes to mind?

TABLE TALK

What's the funniest story you've ever heard about someone getting pulled over by the police while driving?

TABLE TALK

What's the funniest story you've ever heard about someone getting pulled over by the police while driving?

TABLE TALK

Have you ever been called to jury duty? If so, what was it like?

TABLE TALK

Have you ever been called to jury duty? If so, what was it like?

TABLE TALK

If you weren't here at this gathering, where would you be and what would you be doing right now?

TABLE TALK

If you weren't here at this gathering, where would you be and what would you be doing right now?

Session 1: Photocopy this page on plain paper or cardstock, then cut on the dotted lines. Place a set of four cards on each table for Table Talk.

The Lutheran Course Leader Book, copyright © 2005 Augsburg Fortress. May be reproduced for local use.

THE 9.5 THESES

Martin Luther, in the year 1517, wrote 95 Theses (95 statements for debate) which he put on the community bulletin board (the church door) in Wittenberg, Germany. His theses questioned the sale of "indulgences" (written certificates of forgiveness of sins) by church officials. Money from the sale of indulgences was being used to build St. Peter's Basilica in Rome. Here are nine samples of the 95 theses, plus half of one. Do you agree or disagree with each of Luther's points? How would *you* complete thesis 9.5?

1. Our Lord and Master Jesus Christ willed that the whole life of believers should be a life of repentance.
2. Those preachers of indulgences are in error, who say that by the pope's indulgences a person is freed from every penalty, and saved.
3. They preach lies who say that "so soon as the penny jingles into the money-box, the soul flies out [of purgatory]."
4. Every true Christian, whether living or dead, has part in all the blessings of Christ and the Church; and this is granted him by God, even without letters of pardon.
5. Christians are to be taught that he who sees a man in need, and passes him by, and gives [his money] for pardons, purchases not the indulgences of the pope, but the indignation of God.
6. Christians are to be taught that unless they have more than they need, they are bound to keep back what is necessary for their own families, and by no means to squander it on pardons.
7. Christians are to be taught that if the pope knew the exactions of the pardon-preachers, he would rather that St. Peter's church should go to ashes, than that it should be built up with the skin, flesh and bones of his sheep.
8. The true treasure of the Church is the Most Holy Gospel of the glory and the grace of God.
9. Christians are to be exhorted that they be diligent in following Christ, their Head, through penalties, deaths, and hell;

9.5 Christians should be taught that . . .

Session 2: Photocopy this page on plain paper or cardstock.
Place one page on each table for Table Talk.

The Lutheran Course Leader Book, copyright © 2005 Augsburg Fortress.
May be reproduced for local use.

TABLE TALK

What's the most fun you've ever had with water?

TABLE TALK

What's the most fun you've ever had with water?

TABLE TALK

When have you been frightened by water?

TABLE TALK

When have you been frightened by water?

TABLE TALK

Relate an experience you've had with wind and water together.

TABLE TALK

Relate an experience you've had with wind and water together.

TABLE TALK

What is the most beautiful watery place you've ever seen?

TABLE TALK

What is the most beautiful watery place you've ever seen?

Session 3: Photocopy this page on plain paper or cardstock, then cut on the dotted lines. Place a set of four cards on each table for Table Talk.

The Lutheran Course Leader Book, copyright © 2005 Augsburg Fortress. May be reproduced for local use.

TABLE TALK

What does the smell of fresh-baked bread bring to your mind? What is your best memory of bread or bread baking?

TABLE TALK

What does the smell of fresh-baked bread bring to your mind? What is your best memory of bread or bread baking?

TABLE TALK

What meal traditions are special to your family? Thanksgiving? Christmas? Family reunions? What special meals does your family eat together?

TABLE TALK

What meal traditions are special to your family? Thanksgiving? Christmas? Family reunions? What special meals does your family eat together?

TABLE TALK

Do you remember your "First Communion?" How old were you? Who came to share the event with you? What other special events took place at that time? How did you feel about it?

TABLE TALK

Do you remember your "First Communion?" How old were you? Who came to share the event with you? What other special events took place at that time? How did you feel about it?

TABLE TALK

What was, for you, the most meaningful celebration of the Lord's Supper that you recall?

TABLE TALK

What was, for you, the most meaningful celebration of the Lord's Supper that you recall?

Session 4: Photocopy this page on plain paper or cardstock, then cut on the dotted lines. Place a set of cards on each table for Table Talk.

The Lutheran Course Leader Book, copyright © 2005 Augsburg Fortress. May be reproduced for local use.

TABLE TALK

Pass the images of Jesus around the table one at a time and discuss the following questions for each:

- What do you recognize as familiar about Jesus in this image?
- What characteristic or trait of Jesus do you see in this image?
- What aspect of Jesus is surprising or unexpected in this image?

TABLE TALK

Pass the images of Jesus around the table one at a time and discuss the following questions for each:

- What do you recognize as familiar about Jesus in this image?
- What characteristic or trait of Jesus do you see in this image?
- What aspect of Jesus is surprising or unexpected in this image?

TABLE TALK

Pass the images of Jesus around the table one at a time and discuss the following questions for each:

- What do you recognize as familiar about Jesus in this image?
- What characteristic or trait of Jesus do you see in this image?
- What aspect of Jesus is surprising or unexpected in this image?

Session 5: Photocopy this page on plain paper or cardstock, then cut on the dotted lines. Place one card on each table for Table Talk.

The Lutheran Course Leader Book, copyright © 2005 Augsburg Fortress. May be reproduced for local use.

TABLE TALK

So we have the prophetic message more fully confirmed. You will do well to be attentive to this as to a lamp shining in a dark place, until the day dawns and the morning star rises in your hearts. First of all you must understand this, that no prophecy of scripture is a matter of one's own interpretation, because no prophecy ever came by human will, but men and women moved by the Holy Spirit spoke from God (2 Peter 1:19-21).

- What does this passage say to me about the Bible?
- How does this passage challenge me about how I use the Bible?

TABLE TALK

All scripture is inspired by God and is useful for teaching, for reproof, for correction, and for training in righteousness, so that everyone who belongs to God may be proficient, equipped for every good work (2 Timothy 3:16-17).

- What does this passage say to me about the Bible?
- How does this passage challenge me about how I use the Bible?

TABLE TALK

Until I arrive, give attention to the public reading of scripture, to exhorting, to teaching (1 Timothy 4:13).

- What does this passage say to me about the Bible?
- How does this passage challenge me about how I use the Bible?

Session 6: Photocopy this page and the following page on plain paper or cardstock, then cut on the dotted lines. Place one set of cards on each table for Table Talk.

The Lutheran Course Leader Book, copyright © 2005 Augsburg Fortress. May be reproduced for local use. Scripture quotations are from *New Revised Standard Version Bible*, copyright © 1989 Division of Christian Education of the National Council of the Churches of Christ in the United States of America. Used by permission.

TABLE TALK

And [Jesus] rolled up the scroll, gave it back to the attendant, and sat down. The eyes of all in the synagogue were fixed on him. Then he began to say to them, "Today this scripture has been fulfilled in your hearing" (Luke 4:20-21).

- What does this passage say to me about the Bible?
- How does this passage challenge me about how I use the Bible?

TABLE TALK

How sweet are your words to my taste, sweeter than honey to my mouth! Through your precepts I get understanding; therefore I hate every false way. Your word is a lamp to my feet and a light to my path (Psalm 119:103-105).

- What does this passage say to me about the Bible?
- How does this passage challenge me about how I use the Bible?

TABLE TALK

Remember the long way that the LORD your God has led you these forty years in the wilderness, in order to humble you, testing you to know what was in your heart, whether or not you would keep his commandments. He humbled you by letting you hunger, then by feeding you with manna, with which neither you nor your ancestors were acquainted, in order to make you understand that one does not live by bread alone, but by every word that comes from the mouth of the LORD (Deuteronomy 8:2-3).

- What does this passage say to me about the Bible?
- How does this passage challenge me about how I use the Bible?

Session 6: Photocopy this page and the previous page on plain paper or cardstock, then cut on the dotted lines. Place one set of cards on each table for Table Talk.

The Lutheran Course Leader Book, copyright © 2005 Augsburg Fortress. May be reproduced for local use.
Scripture quotations are from *New Revised Standard Version Bible*, copyright © 1989 Division of Christian Education of the National Council of the Churches of Christ in the United States of America. Used by permission.

TABLE TALK

❶ Which of the following approaches represents the style of evangelism with which you would be most comfortable? What experiences have you had with each approach?

- If you die tonight, where will you spend eternity?
- Brothers and sisters, are you saved?
- Please read this brochure; it changed my life.
- If you make a donation in any amount, you can feel sure of God's favor.
- Put your hand on the television! Feel the power we are channeling to you now!
- I think I know something about how you're feeling. Something like that happened to me once, and I didn't know where to turn . . .
- Why don't you come to church with me Sunday? I'll pick you up at 8:30.

❷ Everyone has a faith story. Some are very dramatic. Others seem pretty ordinary. All have God as the "star" character. Where does your faith story begin?

TABLE TALK

❶ Which of the following approaches represents the style of evangelism with which you would be most comfortable? What experiences have you had with each approach?

- If you die tonight, where will you spend eternity?
- Brothers and sisters, are you saved?
- Please read this brochure; it changed my life.
- If you make a donation in any amount, you can feel sure of God's favor.
- Put your hand on the television! Feel the power we are channeling to you now!
- I think I know something about how you're feeling. Something like that happened to me once, and I didn't know where to turn . . .
- Why don't you come to church with me Sunday? I'll pick you up at 8:30.

❷ Everyone has a faith story. Some are very dramatic. Others seem pretty ordinary. All have God as the "star" character. Where does your faith story begin?

Session 7: Photocopy this page on plain paper or cardstock,
then fold in half so that the questions show on the outside. Place one on each table for Table Talk.

The Lutheran Course Leader Book, copyright © 2005 Augsburg Fortress. May be reproduced for local use.

Thank you for taking The Lutheran Course. Please take a few minutes to complete this survey. Your feedback will be used to improve future sessions of the course.

1. The Lutheran Course connected with my daily life.

   Strongly Agree   Agree   Disagree   Strongly Disagree

2. The course helped build positive relationships within my group.

   Strongly Agree   Agree   Disagree   Strongly Disagree

3. My preparation for the sessions took a reasonable amount of time.

   Strongly Agree   Agree   Disagree   Strongly Disagree

4. I will recommend The Lutheran Course to others.

   Strongly Agree   Agree   Disagree   Strongly Disagree

5. I would like to help with future sessions of The Lutheran Course in the following ways. (If interested, check all that apply and provide your name and contact information below.)
   ____Helping with meals or refreshments
   ____Promoting the course
   ____Leading music
   ____Facilitating group discussion
   ____Other: _____

6. Describe the strengths of this course:

7. Describe ways the course could be improved:

8. Any additional comments:

Name _____   E-mail _____
Phone _____

Session 7 Course Evaluation Form: Photocopy for use in the large group.

The Lutheran Course Leader Book, copyright © 2005 Augsburg Fortress. May be reproduced for local use.

www.ingramcontent.com/pod-product-compliance
Lightning Source LLC
Chambersburg PA
CBHW060529010526
44110CB00052B/2546